"In *Simply Pray*, Debbie's clarity and simplicity helped me create a fresh practice of prayer. The principles of Matthew 7:7 to ask, seek, and knock are unfolded with refreshing honesty of how messy our prayers begin, practical applications and tools to bring focus to our prayers, and rich illustrations of answered prayers. If your prayer life needs some CPR to bring back a strong heartbeat, this is the book for you."

—Lisa Allen, Your Confidence Coach, L.J. Allen Coaching

"So many of us feel like absolute failures at prayer. Whether it is our season of life or our attention span that inhibits us, prayer can feel mysterious and strangely hard. Thankfully, Deb Hopper has provided a simple and accessible path forward. With both courageous vulnerability and hard-won faith, Deb is the prayer mentor you have been longing for. If you feel discouraged and stuck, this book is for you!"

—Sharon Hodde Miller, Author of *The Cost of Control*

"Reading *Simply Pray* is like sitting down with the Godly (and fun) wiser woman you've always wanted to take to coffee with your journal in hand as you rapidly take notes, looking up to say, 'But, how?' and 'What if the answer is always *no*?'

"Debbie's personal 'avalanche' led to a powerful prayer life, now resulting in words that fall with the soothing grace and beauty of a fresh, gentle snow. These are the pages I didn't realize I desperately needed to read."

—Kelly Pelfrey, Professional artist and author of *Delight*

"*Simply Pray* is bursting with insightful wisdom, authoritative truth, and powerful testimonies that will pull on your heart strings and increase your faith. Whether you are just dipping your toes into prayer or you've been fully submersed for years, this book will provide you with strategically effective methods to reach the heart of heaven with your prayers."

—Jenna Surratt, Sisterhood pastor, Seacoast Church

"Hebrews tells us that faith does not just believe there is a God but also that He rewards those who earnestly seek Him. You want to believe not just that there is power in prayer but that there is power in *your* prayer. I am a living testimony of this book. I watched an imperfect woman faithfully pray and see God move heaven on my behalf. If you need to know a simple path to increase your faith and, in turn, your prayer life, this is the book for you. It will inspire you to get at Jesus's feet and see Him do some heavy lifting; all you have to do is ASK!"

—Katie Walters, Founder & CEO of Francis + Benedict
and coauthor of *New Marriage, Same Couple*

SIMPLY
PRAY

HOW TO ASK, SEEK, AND KNOCK
FOR ANSWERED PRAYER

DEB HOPPER

Our Daily Bread
Publishing.

Simply Pray: How to Ask, Seek, and Knock for Answered Prayer
© 2024 by Deb Hopper

Requests for permission to quote from this book should be directed to: Permissions Department, Our Daily Bread Publishing, PO Box 3566, Grand Rapids, MI 49501, or contact us by email at permissionsdept@odb.org.

The author is represented by Tom Dean, Literary Agent with A Drop of Ink LLC, www.adropofink.pub.

Scripture quotations, unless otherwise indicated, are taken from the Holy Bible, New International Version®, NIV®. Copyright © 1973, 1978, 1984, 2011 by Biblica, Inc.™ Used by permission of Zondervan. All rights reserved worldwide. zondervan.com.
    Scripture quotations marked AMP are taken from the Amplified® Bible, Copyright © 2015 by The Lockman Foundation. Used by permission. www.Lockman.org.
    Scripture quotations marked ESV are taken from the ESV® Bible (The Holy Bible, English Standard Version®), copyright © 2001 by Crossway, a publishing ministry of Good News Publishers. Used by permission. All rights reserved.
    Scripture quotations marked MSG are taken from *The Message*, copyright © 1993, 2002, 2018 by Eugene H. Peterson. Used by permission of NavPress, represented by Tyndale House Publishers. All rights reserved.
    Scripture quotations marked NET are from the NET Bible® copyright © 1996, 2019 by Biblical Studies Press, L.L.C. All rights reserved. Scripture quoted by permission. http://netbible.com.
    Scripture quotations marked NLT are taken from the Holy Bible, New Living Translation, copyright © 1996, 2004, 2015 by Tyndale House Foundation. Used by permission of Tyndale House Publishers, Inc., Carol Stream, Illinois 60188. All rights reserved.

Interior design by Michael J. Williams

ISBN: 978-1-64070-262-2

Library of Congress Cataloging-in-Publication Data Available

Printed in the United States of America
24 25 26 27 28 29 30 31 / 8 7 6 5 4 3 2 1

Dedicated to single moms everywhere who are feeling overwhelmed and burdened with raising a family alone. May these words be a reminder that God sees you, He loves you, and He hears your prayers.

She gave this name to the LORD who spoke to her: "You are the God who sees me," for she said, "I have now seen the One who sees me."

GENESIS 16:13

CONTENTS

Part Four: Seeing God in the Answers

FOREWORD

Prayer is wild.

It's mysterious and also as close as our breath.

It's the act of talking to our Father, the one who created and sustains the universe . . . but it's also just honest words.

I can be a naturally doubtful and dubious kind of gal, but I've never really gone through a faltering season of faith when it comes to prayer.

And that I credit to having a mother who prayed.

I saw the telltale signs of her time with God as I was growing up. I'd notice the journal and the half-full coffee mug on a coffee table in the morning. I heard her at the kitchen table, in front of others, in private, on hard days, and on the best days—earnestly talking to her Father and thanking Him for listening. She laid hands on us when we were sick, encouraged us to pause and pray on the morning of our weddings. She spoke in muttered words during the most mundane and miraculous moments of my life.

She prayed. And she counted the fruit as she saw evidence that her Father listened, even when others didn't see it that way.

For most of my adult life, my friends have longingly expressed some lighthearted jealousy regarding my mom and our relationship. And I get it, because she's incredible.

So while I'm not open to sharing her as a mom, it is my great joy to introduce you to this kind guide and wise mentor, who I believe will help you feel more free and fulfilled in your prayer life.

She knows that prayer is a mystery, but she's going to encourage you to start to grow in simple and practical ways. She's going to tell you some of those stories that have built her faith, and certainly mine, as we've seen God do what He does over and over again.

You're not going to leave this book feeling the same about prayer.

You're not going to leave this book feeling the same about your Father.

You are going to finish the book knowing you're so equipped to speak our native language.

Because you can simply pray and see your whole world change.

Enjoy my mom and her wild wisdom—I get her back for Sunday lunch!

Jess Connolly
Author of *You Are the Girl for the Job*,
Breaking Free from Body Shame,
and *Tired of Being Tired*

AT THE BOTTOM
OF AN AVALANCHE

Matthew 7:7 saved me from a deep, dark place during a lonely time in my life.

My ten-year marriage had ended, and I found myself buried under a massive weight as a single mother with primary custody of two girls, ages three and six. Divorce had never been in my family and certainly not in any vision I had for my life. My parents' marriage and others I'd observed didn't seem perfect, but they stayed together. Not mine. Mine toppled like an *avalanche*—"a sudden great or overwhelming rush or accumulation of something."[1] Yes, that's what it felt like. An overwhelming rush and accumulation of some things.

So taken by this definition, I wondered what signs scientists look for before an avalanche. I googled, and this is what I found:

> An avalanche occurs when the snowpack—or the layers of accumulated snow—on the side of a mountain is in some way disturbed, leading to a fracturing of the top layer and a downward torrent of a large mass of the white stuff. . . .
> A number of factors can set off a disturbance.[2]

A number of factors can set off a disturbance . . . That sounded familiar.

I won't go into detail about the stormy seasons of our marriage, the fracturing, or the factors that contributed to the avalanche. Because when you're faced with an avalanche, you're not analyzing what you should have done. All you care about is survival.

That's how I found myself: single again at thirty-one and trying to survive. Between driving two girls to school and making a sixty-mile round-trip commute to work each day, I was busy and overwhelmed. There was no time to assess the collateral damage or determine why it happened.

The Rescue

Thankfully, my good friend Kay Johnson Smith was not afraid to speak hard truths. She asked me to lunch one day and said gently but firmly, "Debbie, you've got to get a grip. Your life is a mess, and it's time you made some changes." I don't remember any other details of that day except my ugly cry.

The next day Kay called and said, "I told you it's time to make some changes in your life, but I didn't give you the key to making those changes." It helped that this friend had also walked the same path of divorce and single parenting and was a few years ahead of me. She seemed to be not only surviving but thriving. So I was paying attention.

Kay then told me how to apply the principle of prayer found in Matthew 7:7: ask, seek, and knock. The way she had learned it was to write out the verse on one side of several index cards: "Ask and it will be given to you; seek and you will find; knock and the door will be opened to you." She told me to write the one thing I was praying about on the reverse side and post the cards everywhere I would see them daily. On the refrigerator, mirrors, car dashboard, or kitchen cabinets. But I was to tape them so that only the verse was visible. The simple act of doing this would focus me on praying (asking, seeking, knocking) and release the area needing prayer to God.

This sounded easy enough, but I didn't know which area of my life to focus on first. I was getting buried deeper and deeper under discouragement and frustration. Here are the CliffsNotes of my life at that point:

House: My first husband and I moved to a much smaller, older house needing major renovations. But just a few months after moving in, our marriage ended—leaving me alone with a home that had uneven floors, baseboard heat, and a lot of maintenance. Forty-five minutes away from family and support systems in Charlotte, North Carolina, it no longer seemed the best location for the girls and me.

Job: I was working for a nonprofit and loved the work and culture but had a forty-minute commute each way and limited salary and benefits. The commute was also not good for a single mom who needed more flexibility in her days.

Body: During the separation, I had given in to emotional eating and gained thirty pounds.

Car: My car had died two weeks before Christmas and was so badly broken I'd just left it on the side of the road. Now driving a twenty-year-old pickup truck of my dad's and commuting sixty miles a day to and from work, I knew that a reliable car was a priority.

The Index Cards

That weekend, the girls and I went with my parents to the beach for a getaway. I had time by myself and walked the beach, crying out, "God, I don't even know which area of my life to pray about first. I know the exercise is meant to focus on one area, but I have four areas needing your help. I can't narrow it down to just one. It's all a mess." As I walked that beach and screamed out from under the weight of my circumstances, it became clear that all four areas needed change and forward movement: house, job, body, car.

Once home, I pulled out index cards and wrote Matthew 7:7 on each one. Then I flipped one over and wrote "House." On another I wrote "Job." Next came "Body" and then "Car." I taped these index cards all over our little shack, on the dashboard of my dad's truck, on

15

mirrors and refrigerators, and then I began the process of focusing on that passage and releasing the areas to God.

While it felt a little silly to tape those index cards everywhere, a peace did come over me as I focused on the verse: "Ask and it will be given to you; seek and you will find; knock and the door will be opened to you." On a few cards, I just wrote "Ask Seek Knock." Then, after a few weeks of repeating the phrase, I realized the acronym of those three words was ASK. So on some cards I wrote "A-S-K," but under my breath I would repeat the whole verse until it became part of my mind, soul, and spirit.

My first step in reaching up toward life began with my simple prayers of ask, seek, and knock.

In those days of survival, I didn't have a deep theology of what it meant to ask God, to seek Him, or to keep knocking. My understanding of how God listens developed over the years as He taught me more about prayer. I didn't think it was some magical formula just so that I could receive, like a genie in a bottle. But when I was at the bottom of an avalanche, in survival mode, there was something beautiful in believing that my first step in reaching up toward life began with my simple prayers of ask, seek, and knock.

Applying Matthew 7:7

What I experienced in my first experiment of ASK was that it was anything but a passive journey. In my simplistic cry for help and a solution to the overwhelming collateral damage, I didn't know what the next steps should be. I needed to put one foot in front of the other, much like if I had lost muscular ability in my legs and was using a walker to rebuild muscles.

My father had many health problems in his mid-fifties, the most traumatic being the amputation of his left leg. He was eventually fitted with a prosthetic leg but then had to learn to walk all over again. Dad's physical therapy included using a walker to help move the immobile prosthetic forward in some type of rhythmic concert with his right leg, which had forgotten how to move properly. His walker was a prop, needed just long enough to retrain the good leg and provide stability for the new leg.

In my early days of praying and asking, the index cards were my walker. They trained my faith to focus on hope for each situation and God's promises until I could build faith muscles of my own with a deeper knowledge of God than just ask, seek, and knock. As I began to build faith muscles, prayer allowed me to grip the metal frame of God's truth and believe that if I just held on, He would build these muscles. Once my muscles were strengthened, God would show me how to take the next steps in at least one of the four areas I had written on the back of each card.

What I experienced in my first practice of Matthew 7:7 was that God heard and cared about my circumstances. Within thirty days of praying "ask, seek, and knock," I was moving ahead in two of the four areas. Here's how God walked me through the next few months while I was praying for direction and yielding to His answers.

God Listens

In month one, there were no quick fixes or answers, so I simply prayed and released anxiety about the four areas. However, the quickest answered prayer was about my car. Two weeks into my Matthew 7:7 journey, I noticed an advertisement in the newspaper for new cars at a Nissan dealership with a rebate offer that could be applied as a down payment. Since I had no savings and no car to trade in, this was a great solution. Within a few days I was driving a Nissan Sentra. Answered prayer number one!

During the second month, I felt prompted to reach out to a former employer. This VP had always told me I could return if circumstances changed, so I called to tell him that I needed a higher salary and better benefits. His reply shocked me. He told me that he was working on a new management position and would love to see me in that role, but it would take several months to be approved.

In the third month, a woman from Charlotte came to me with a unique offer. Instead of making a full-price offer on my house, she would take it as is, with the repairs needed, for a lesser price and I could rent her three-bedroom townhome at a lower monthly rate. Her townhome was in a Charlotte school district where the girls could attend elementary school just five minutes from my parents' house, where they could walk after school. Answered prayer number two!

In the fourth month, I looked into more options for a diet program with accountability, but even with discounts, the cost was $200. (This was before gyms and online workouts.) Because I was moving, the gas company mailed me a check that month for the propane remaining in the tank. It was $212, almost exactly the amount I needed to sign up. I enrolled with my friend and started new healthy eating habits.

In the fifth month, I continued the new eating plan and lost the extra weight. Answered prayer number three!

In month six, my former VP called with a job offer. The position was tailor-made for my skills and started at almost $8,000 over my current salary. Answered prayer number four!

God Answers

It was now the summer, and I had experienced answered prayers for each of the four areas that I had written on the Matthew 7:7 index cards in January. House, job, body, car. Each area required asking, seeking, and knocking. Where I had previously been stuck, my life now had forward movement. What I later learned is that some of these answered prayers also changed my life and impacted my family for generations to come.

If our prayers can have that kind of influence, shouldn't we spend more time exploring the subject? In the following pages, I'll break down my prayer journey of the past thirty-five years, from taking baby steps to what has evolved into a continuous prayer life.

Whether you are dipping your toe into the water of prayer for the first time, wanting clarity for uncharted waters of your prayer life, or surfing the waves of God's answered prayers, I hope you'll jump in!

PART ONE

ASK

CHAPTER 1

ASK LIKE A CHILD

Have you heard a child crying for help when they've been hurt? If the child can't verbalize where they're hurting or what happened, they're only able to give the most piercing screams. A parent might try to coax the child into an explanation, but usually reassurance and comfort are the first step.

After my avalanche of divorce, I was like that crying child as I wobbled into this adventure called prayer. No one was teaching me how to take those first baby steps of single-again life, but some childlike qualities of my faith—especially trust in my Father's care—were much needed for effective praying. I knew I was immobilized and needed help.

It's important at this early point in our journey to shake off any preconceived notions about God and look at prayer from a child's view. A child's favorite question is "Why?" Here are three reasons why we can and should *ask like a child*.

God Can Be Trusted

I realize now, with many decades of hindsight, what made it easier for me to ask in my initial application of Matthew 7:7 was the childlike innocence of my faith. Although I had grown up in the church, much of my spiritual awakening to this point had taken place at youth group camps and summer revivals. Without any deep dive into God's Word or the Bible studies that came later in my life, I had basic beliefs that had been formed in the pews singing "The Old Rugged Cross" and "Amazing Grace." Thankfully, the one area of my faith that wasn't too complicated or messy was my belief in a powerful and all-loving God.

Starting with trust may seem oversimplified since we likely all agree that we can and should trust God. But after years of counseling women in the church, I know many times we compare God to our earthly fathers, which limits our understanding of His power and our trust in Him, and sometimes even perverts our perception of God's abilities. Instead of man being created in God's image, we subconsciously reverse the order by assigning qualities of fallen men to the creator God, our Father.

> So God created mankind in his own image,
>   in the image of God he created them;
>   male and female he created them. (Genesis 1:27)

Knowing who God is and remembering that as our Creator He is all-powerful may help us approach Him with bold asks, but it doesn't automatically build trust. Trust is a tricky thing if you've been disappointed by humans, which has a one-hundred-percent probability if you're depending on people. We all disappoint, and we all have been disappointed. It's the nature of being human in a fallen world. So even in our prayers, stating the obvious that God is worthy of our trust as we talk to Him reminds us not to compare Him to any earthly representation. King David knew this and repeated it often. When my trust factor is low, I start praying with these words from the Psalms to remind my soul that God can be trusted:

> In you, LORD my God,
>   I put my trust. (25:1)

> But I trust in you, LORD;
>> I say, "You are my God." (31:14)

> In God I trust and am not afraid.
>> What can man do to me? (56:11)

God Is Listening

As I think about asking like a child, it helps to remember that God is listening and really wants His best for me. Jeremiah 29:11 is framed as art in many nurseries for a reason: "For I know the plans I have for you, declares the LORD, plans for welfare and not for evil, to give you a future and a hope" (ESV). This promise reassures every parent of a newborn that there is a bright future for their child. Later in life, it's also comforting to us when our current trajectory doesn't feel bright or hopeful. I need reminding that God has good plans for my future right now—not just when I'm an infant. We all need "a future and a hope" in different seasons, and if this is one of those seasons for you, I encourage you to hold on to this promise.

I find it interesting, though, that we don't see the following verse cross-stitched or framed as much as verse 11: "Then you will call upon me and come and pray to me, and I will hear you" (v. 12 ESV). It's reassuring to know that God not only has plans for my future but is telling me to come pray and He will listen.

When first beginning this journey into prayer during my early thirties, I called out much like a child asks her father for help in a time of need. Before I learned to be too sophisticated with my asks, these requests of house, job, body, and car were the most urgent things I needed to get me unstuck and moving forward. Isn't that just like a child? When children want something for their birthday or Christmas, they note the item or give a list, without conditions or any thought about eternal value.

My grandchild Abel modeled this well. I dubbed him "the gift whisperer" because when he wanted something, he would whisper it into my ear often as a hint. Even if we were far from a celebration that might get him the desire of his heart, he'd start to research said item and then talk to me about ways he could earn the money to purchase it. By whispering about the item frequently, he let me know that it was important enough to consume his every waking hour. When I heard the first whispers, it prompted me to ask questions. Why did he want it? What joy would this item bring? Were there any substitutes or work-arounds that were less expensive? As his Nonny, I wanted to help him get the item he wanted. I loved his heart and the fact that he would work to make it happen once he knew that I was more than just an open wallet.

God is listening, God is paying attention, and, most importantly, God cares about the details of my life.

My early Matthew 7:7 prayers to the Father were much like the gift whisperer's reminders to me. Because what comes with a child's request is an intrinsic trust that someone is listening. My first experience with the 7:7 principle proved to me that God is listening, God is paying attention, and, most importantly, God cares about the details of my life.

God Gives Us Good Things

Another unique instruction in the ask, seek, and knock passage in Matthew 7 almost demands that we ask as a child when we pray. The section following verse 7 gives us the following proposition:

> Which of you, if your son asks for bread, will give him a stone? Or if he asks for a fish, will give him a snake? If you, then, though you are evil, know how to give good gifts to your children, how much more will your Father in heaven give good gifts to those who ask him! (Matthew 7:9–11)

This set of questions provides the assumption that we are the children and God is the Father. The well-known English preacher Charles Spurgeon notes this about the stone: "There were many stones in those days that were in appearance wonderfully like the bread which they used in the East; but would any father mock his son by giving him one of those stones to break his teeth on, instead of bread that he could eat? Never."[3]

But sometimes, because another human has given us a stone for bread, we forget that God is the perfect Father and would never give us what the world has casually tossed our way.

In the case of the gift whisperer, Abel one time wanted a set of Apple AirPods for his gaming setup. He had whispered, and I was listening. After all, I owned a set of AirPods and believed them to be one of the best products ever made. But the cost was over a hundred dollars, and the whisperer had only thirty dollars saved. Lest you doubt his convincing approach, he'd even gotten his older sister talking about buying him AirPods for Christmas when she didn't own any herself!

Like the thrifty, cost-saving, budgeting Nonny I am, I searched for a substitute that might satisfy this twelve-year-old and his need for wireless AirPods. In a clearance store I found a substitute brand for only twenty dollars and purchased them on the spot. When I got home, I charged them and tried them out—but only one earbud worked. When I finally researched the brand, the reviews confirmed this faulty product. But since they were clearance and I couldn't return them, I gave them to the gift whisperer in hopes that one was better than none.

This is just one example of an earthly father or Nonny who tried to give good gifts but was no representation of our heavenly Father. So I might paraphrase that verse: "Which of you, if your grandson asks for Apple AirPods, would give him a knockoff brand that only has one working? Not God!" (Matthew 7:9–11 Nonny Version).

God Has a Plan

Another way we can ask like a child is trusting in the sovereignty of God and not trying to control or determine the outcome. As an overachiever, I feel confident most days I can make something happen. That strength can sometimes be twisted into manipulation or control.

One ask where I totally trusted in God's plan and am ever grateful that my base nature was pushed down began eight years into my single-again life. I was praying for remarriage and my forever husband. I had been happily single for several years but still felt an emptiness and a desire to be married. After trying to figure this out on my own through singles groups, dating apps (well, let's be honest, they were magazines then, not apps), and dating setups by well-meaning friends, I went to God. A nearby church sponsored a workshop titled "The Things That Really Matter" and guided us in making a top-ten list of the things that should matter in choosing a spouse. I spent several days composing my list, and after praying over it, I tucked it away and forgot about it. A year later I met my forever husband, Gibson, and knew he was the one God had for me.

A month before our wedding, I was flipping through my Bible and found a scribbled piece of paper with my "Top Ten Things That Really Matter" in a future husband. Gibson matched all ten things on the list. I had not thought about the list since penning it, praying over it, and tucking it into my Bible. What a great reminder that God didn't forget my request but is sovereign over the circumstances of my life. I began praising God at that moment, and have continued every day since, for how He answered my prayer in choosing and arranging for Gibson and me to get married over twenty-eight years ago. Sometimes asking like a child means whispering your desires to God, tucking the list away, and trusting that He is still at work on the solution.

> Trust in the LORD with all your heart,
>   and do not lean on your own understanding.
> In all your ways acknowledge him,
>   and he will make straight your paths. (Proverbs
>   3:5–6 ESV)

This is how you ask like a child. Trust (with all your heart), lean (on Him, not on your understanding of things), and submit to God, and the result will be straight paths. It doesn't take too many episodes of falling all by yourself before you learn that it's easier to trust and lean on someone stronger.

Over the years as I added more ASKs before the Lord using the Matthew 7:7 principle, I had His answers to build my weak faith. This one Bible verse was like my Father leaning down to give me His fingers for balance, so I could hold on and keep from stumbling until I could lean on other promises and a deeper understanding of my heavenly Father. He was building strong prayer muscles in me one step at a time.

As children grow into their teens and then mature into young adults, they face the temptation to become too wise for their own good. Those of us who remember our early twenties can recall a time when we seemed to know more than our parents. Over time, as our knowledge and experience grow, we learn that our old childlike innocence and wonder can become some of the greatest strengths we will possess in life.

As we progress and learn more about going to the next level of asking in the following chapters, let's take one wobbly baby step with complete trust and keep our eyes on the One who is leading the way.

ASK in Your Life

1. What are you ASKing God for today?

2. If prayer isn't your first response when the questions of life pop up, post Matthew 7:7 so you'll be reminded to *simply pray*. Put it on index cards or as the wallpaper of your phone or laptop. Do you spend time in the kitchen or on your treadmill? At the office or in the car? Post it in all the places where you'll see it regularly until prayer becomes your go-to response to the everyday and the not-so-everyday.

3. How do your prayers need to change in order to ask, seek, and knock like a child?

4. Memorize Psalm 25:1, 31:14, or 56:11 (see pages 24–25) so you can pray it to God.

CHAPTER 2

ASK ANYTHING AND EVERYTHING

One thing my first venture into utilizing the ASK model of prayer did was to build up my confidence to ask for *anything*. God had shown clear answers or opened doors for me in each area of house, job, body, and car, giving me the assurance that He heard my prayers and cared about the details of my life. And as I studied more about prayer, the following verses made exactly what I should ask for quite clear.

> And *whatever* you ask in prayer, you will receive, if you have faith. (Matthew 21:22 ESV, emphasis added)

> Therefore I tell you, *whatever* you ask in prayer, believe that you have received it, and it will be yours. (Mark 11:24 ESV, emphasis added)

The last time I checked, the definition of *whatever* was "anything or everything."[4]

These two verses in Matthew and Mark follow after the time Jesus cursed the fig tree and all its leaves withered. Many scholars believe this was an object lesson on two counts: the fruitfulness of believers and their faithfulness in prayer. While the disciples were amazed at the suddenly withered fig tree, Jesus turned this miracle into a teachable moment with his "whatever" statement:

> And Jesus answered them, "Truly, I say to you, if you have faith and do not doubt, you will not only do what has been done to the fig tree, but even if you say to this mountain, 'Be taken up and thrown into the sea,' it will happen. And *whatever* you ask in prayer, you will receive, if you have faith." (Matthew 21:21–22 ESV, emphasis added)

As I studied these passages over the next years, it became clear that praying for anything that is on my heart and mind is okay if I ask with enough faith to believe God can do it. And not just praying that God will fix my refrigerator or help me find a parking space, though I've been known to do that on a hot low-country day. Family moves and where to live have also been important topics for prayer.

When we moved to the area of Charleston, South Carolina, my husband had lined up ten houses for us to see in one day with a real estate agent. I had been praying that God would show me the exact house that would become our home, because the process seemed overwhelming. Without knowing the city or neighborhoods, I didn't want to choose a house just based on the number of bedrooms or baths. So as I prayed for clarity about the house God had for us, I also had faith that He would show us exactly where to live. It wasn't until we saw the tenth house that I knew. It was a spec house. The frames were in but no windows. As we walked in the front door, the wind blew through, and I felt the Holy Spirit whispering, *This is the one.* Gibson and the agent were both confused because the previous house we had seen just one street away was larger and grander for almost the same price. But I loved this house on Great Hope Drive. Even the name of the street seemed a divine affirmation. I remembered a passage in Hebrews 3:6 that reminds us, "We are his house, if indeed we hold firmly to our confidence and the hope in which we glory." I couldn't imagine living anywhere except on Great Hope.

So my prayers continued to grow in faith, and they certainly agreed with the "whatevers" in Matthew 21 and Mark 11. But even in our childlike prayers, it's important to keep learning about other passages that teach us about praying for "whatever."

Asking in His Will

Interpreting God's will is a slippery slope, because who can really know the will of God, creator of the universe?

In one of his letters, the apostle John teaches Christians how to pray: "And this is the confidence that we have toward him, that if we ask anything according to his will he hears us. And if we know that he hears us in whatever we ask, we know that we have the requests that we have asked of him" (1 John 5:14–15 ESV).

Put more simply, Bible teacher Adrian Rogers says in his article "Prayer and the Will of God": "Do you fear what God's will for you might be? I'll let you in on a secret: The will of God for you is what you would want if you knew everything from God's viewpoint!"[5]

When my mom's time on earth seemed to be dwindling, I had talked to enough of her doctors and done enough research to know her last days would be unimaginably painful. Mother had pulmonary fibrosis, Parkinson's disease, and congestive heart failure. If any of those three terminal illnesses continued to debilitate her eighty-one-year-old body, her last days would be spent gasping for air or with muscles twisted in pain.

My mother had the purest and sweetest spirit, with a kind word and smile for all those who came near. My prayer for her became simply, "God, please let her die in her sleep. I can't imagine that it's in Your will for her to suffer or to be in pain when there's no cure or remedy for the diseases ravaging her body. Take her in her sleep."

One Sunday, my daughter Jess, my granddaughter Glory, and I went to visit Nana. She had been recovering from a recent hospitalization with pneumonia, doing more damage to her fragile lungs. She was sitting up in her recliner, watching a Hallmark movie, and hugged me, saying, "Thank you for all you've done to take care of me."

The next morning, her senior home called early to say that they had found her unresponsive when they went to wake her for breakfast. God had taken her home peacefully in her sleep. I believe that was His will for my mother.

My mother died at eighty-one years of age when my ultimate wish would have been for her to live to one hundred. She only met nine of her sixteen great-grandchildren, but she would've loved to watch all of them grow up. She was at weddings for three of her six grands but would've danced at every one, she adored them so much. She didn't live long enough to see me preach or minister or write this book, fulfilling many of the dreams she knew were in my heart. So of course my selfish prayers would've been for her to share many more years with all of us. But praying God's will for her life's end was releasing her to heaven to a life without pain instead of keeping her in a declining physical body.

Are there situations in your life you might be praying about which seem *good* but maybe aren't *best* from God's perspective? How do we move from good to best? Are your prayers lining up with the longer view or simply short-term solutions? Do your asks have any personal agenda attached to them? Searching my heart and releasing control of the outcome is one thing I've found helpful to filter out self-centered prayers. Studying more about the lives of other Jesus followers, especially the first disciples, helps me keep an eternal perspective when my prayers are filled with earthly asks. Sometimes praying aloud with another person, or asking for counsel about your prayer, is enough to put a spotlight on any requests that might not line up with God's will.

Asking in His Name

Another verse that uses the same Greek word for "whatever" or "anything" (*ti*) as in 1 John 5:14–15 helps us understand another aspect about asking God for anything:

Whatever you ask in my name, this I will do, that the Father may be glorified in the Son. (John 14:13 ESV, emphasis added)

So asking whatever in this verse also adds the caveat of asking in Jesus's name. I've heard people pray this way before, haven't you? They say, "In the name of Jesus," or "In Jesus's name," or "Jesus, we pray this in your name." Is that what John meant? Surely we are not supposed to just qualify anything we ask for by adding those words to our prayers. As my study Bible notes about John 14:13: "Praying in Jesus' name means praying in a way consistent with his character and his will (a person's name in the ancient world represented what the person was like). . . . Effective prayer must ask for and desire what Jesus delights in."[6]

A helpful analogy for praying in Jesus's name comes from old movies. When a police officer says, "Stop in the name of the law!" the implication is that the officer is speaking with the approval of a greater power. Or a foreign ambassador might say, "I agree to these terms in the name of the king." It means that the ruler has given the ambassador the authority to make such a bargain. In both cases, they would only request things that line up with the law or power they represent. Similarly, we should feel confident in praying for anything that lines up with Jesus's law or teachings.

Asking and Abiding

How do we know what Jesus delights in? I like to compare this to knowing what one of my girlfriends delights in. One way I am able to know what my friends delight in is by spending time with them on a regular basis. If I only see a friend once a year, I have less chance of knowing about the little things that delight her than if I spend time with that person observing her preferences and taking note of what brings her joy. One friend and I have a routine of walking through a home-goods store after we meet for lunch. Watching her pick up a certain candle or napkin gives me clues about her color preferences.

Even her selection of serving dishes or cookware tells me about how she prepares for holidays or family gatherings. When we talk about trials or difficult situations we are walking through, her solution always points back to God's truths. Spending time with her, observing and listening, shows me what she delights in.

In yet one more verse of asking for "whatever," we get more understanding about how to find out what Jesus delights in: "If you abide in me, and my words abide in you, ask whatever you wish, and it will be done for you" (John 15:7 ESV). By abiding with Jesus, spending time getting to know Him and learning about what delights Him, we are better equipped to ask for "whatever" in our prayers. The second part of the verse says "and my words abide in you," which further tells me to spend time soaking deeply in His Word (the Bible) until those words are part of my vocabulary, part of my thinking. Just like I know my girlfriends better if I spend time with them and listen to them, if I abide with Jesus and His words are in me, my asks will more naturally line up with what delights Him.

Whenever I've prayed something for a long time and I'm wondering whether it's really what Jesus desires or delights in, I ask myself two questions about the prayer request:

1. If Jesus were standing in front of me, would I ask Him this prayer?
2. Is there any way this prayer is selfish or only going to benefit me?

This might be a little simplistic, and it certainly would be better if we were just abiding in Him and letting His words and teachings become part of us before we prayed for whatever. But it does help me root out some selfish prayers.

Anything Is Everything

As the mother of three adult daughters, I'm usually asked every holiday what I'd like to have as a present. Every time my answer is the gift of time. "I'd love a lunch or time with the three of you." That's not a simple ask because they are busy women with full-time careers and ministry demands, not to mention eleven children between them. But I think I've answered them enough times with the same answer because the past couple of years they've succeeded in making my wishes come true.

A few years ago for my birthday and Mother's Day (which happened to fall on the same week), my daughters planned a night at a local beach resort with time for walking, talking, and dinner. The next year they planned a two-day trip for the four of us.

Knowing that I want time and conversation with them more than anything else they could give me reminds me of my relationship with God. When I pray, it's not as critical for me to get the requests right. God just wants a conversation with me. He wants to hear my heart, my fears and concerns, and my deepest wishes. If I ask for my dishwasher to be fixed or a child to be healed, I'm being honest and true about my current longing. Asking my heavenly Father for anything means I can ask Him for everything, even when I don't get it right.

God just wants a conversation with me. He wants to hear my heart, my fears and concerns, and my deepest wishes.

Ultimately, God knows that our hearts are sinful and that sometimes we are going to pray for things that don't line up with His will or aren't in His timing. Yet asking anything tells God that we trust Him; we are coming to Him as children to our Father and depending on His power and strength instead of our own. Anything is everything when you remain in a childlike position before Father God. When we enter into a relationship with our Abba Father, we are heirs to an inheritance that is anything and everything: "The Spirit you received does not make you slaves, so that you live in fear again; rather, the Spirit you received brought about your adoption to sonship. And by him we cry, '*Abba*, Father.' The Spirit himself testifies with our spirit that we are God's children" (Romans 8:15–16).

In future chapters, I share examples of how asking for anything includes prayers for healing, prayers for direction, prayers for protection from disease or illness, and prayers for career moves. The point of sharing these is not to give a list of acceptable things to pray for but to underscore how we as children can come to our heavenly Father with anything and everything that is on our hearts. Understanding this principle is foundational to all the other building blocks of prayer. Asking only matters when you believe that you can talk to God about anything . . . and that means everything.

ASK in Your Life

1. What is a "whatever" you've been hesitating to ask God for? Something that might seem insignificant in light of eternity but is important to you?
2. Which of your prayers may be selfish instead of in God's will? Partner with a trusted friend in prayer and get feedback on how your prayers line up with His Word.
3. How confident are you that you're a child of God? Read over Romans 8:15–16 until you can cry out, "*Abba*, Father."
4. Ignoring any human misrepresentations of fatherhood, try having a conversation with the only perfect Father, who is waiting for you to talk to Him.

CHAPTER 3

ASK AND RECEIVE MORE

About five years after my first journey of applying the Matthew 7:7 principle, I got specific in praying for the future spouses of my two oldest daughters. I prayed, "Lord, please let these girls follow you the rest of their lives. I pray their marriages would be strong and healthy—and while you're at it, Lord, can you have them marry pastors?"

Maybe that doesn't seem like such a big ask, but remember, I was raising these two girls as a single mom with all the wounds and scars of divorce. Both daughters had exhibited rebellion, but I believed in a God who could beat the odds. You see, the odds for children of divorce say that they are 35 percent more likely to have a divorce of their own.[7] I wanted more for my daughters and believed that anything was possible if I just asked. Sons-in-law who are pastors may not be the best prayer request for everyone, but I knew my daughters needed marriages with men who were strong in the Lord. Silly me. God honored my request but probably was laughing with the angels since He knew that pastoring is one of the toughest assignments on earth. I absolutely adore my two sons-in-law and cannot imagine better spouses for Katie and Jess. But the joke was on me since they each did not just marry a pastor but also received a strong call from God on their lives to become preachers of His Word. They each co-pastor with Josh and Nick in their churches but also have ministries of their own.

Since being a woman pastor had been off-limits to me in the 1970s as a career path, I couldn't imagine asking for my daughters to serve God in that way. There was a beauty in this prayer when God answered with more than I could ask or imagine.

Land of the Big God

My daughters entering ministry is a perfect example of what I later learned is promised in Ephesians 3:20: "Now to him who is able to do immeasurably more than all we ask or imagine, according to his power that is at work within us . . ." That "immeasurably more" underscores the big God we are asking and how He sometimes answers our limited prayers with more.

Sometimes, though, we don't dream big dreams or ask God for more because we forget who we are praying to. Are we addressing our prayers to someone who is on our own human level or someone powerful enough to raise the dead to life? This seems to be the question behind many of our human cries for help. Paul reminds us that God's power is mightier than anything we can fathom, as He raised Jesus from the dead: ". . . and his incomparably great power for us who believe. That power is the same as the mighty strength he exerted when he raised Christ from the dead and seated him at his right hand in the heavenly realms" (Ephesians 1:19–20). Too often we ask based on our limited perspective, our limited scope of who God is.

A friend of ours and regional leader for sub-Saharan Africa for Pioneers International, Pastor Francis Avoyi, often tells us that Africa is a land of "the big God" while America is a land of "the little God." Pastor Francis believes this because he sees Togolese people in great need going before God with great asks, while Americans are in less need and therefore ask less in our prayers. But even if we are asking less in our prayers, I'm thankful those will be multiplied when presented to a big God.

How are you addressing God in your prayers? Do you pray to someone who is a big God or a little God? I can certainly agree with Pastor Francis that when my needs are greater, my prayers are exponentially bigger. Have you experienced the same? Will shifting your perspective of Him change the scope of your prayers? I'm grateful that even when I pray little prayers, a big God is listening and able to provide more than I can ask. *God's answers to my prayers are usually better than what I can ask or imagine.*

Our Daily Bread

One area where I've prayed and received more than I can ask or imagine is in finances and provision. I've worked jobs since I was fourteen years old and full-time since twenty-one to help pay my way through college. Most years, I was praying for "daily bread" as taught by Jesus in the Lord's Prayer (Matthew 6:9–13). I never dreamed of or prayed for abundance. Rather, I thought I would work full-time until Jesus called me home, and I don't remember ever thinking or praying that there'd be surplus. This mindset came partly from growing

God's answers to my prayers are usually better than what I can ask or imagine.

up in a feast-or-famine environment. My dad owned his own company, and we never saw huge benefits from that ownership, just the financial hardships.

Enter my thirties, when I was trying to survive as a single mom, living paycheck to paycheck. There were plenty of times I prayed for wisdom about how to pay monthly bills or how to feed my family. My second marriage at age thirty-nine brought the blessing of a second income, but we were also starting over financially during the most expensive years of raising teenagers with cars, followed by college and weddings. We incurred a lot of debt in those years and even with good earnings, continued to just make ends meet. Even with diligence toward our finances over the last decade, God's answer to a prayer for daily bread has meant gracious provision. From the young woman who only envisioned working full-time until Jesus called me home to becoming self-employed in my mid-sixties, God continues to amaze me with more than I could ask or imagine.

Vision Given to the Daughters

Another example of how He has answered prayers more than I could ask or imagine is with my grandchildren. I grew up in a family of three children and nine cousins, so holidays and vacations were full and fun. But in my first marriage, when it seemed at first as if I couldn't conceive, I didn't pray for a large family. The vision for a family where cousins grew up knowing one another and loving time at their grandparents was planted deep in my soul, but it was not something I prayed about. Instead, I prayed for one or two children, who might then have a couple of children of their own. The eighties were a time of family planning, so nothing in our culture led us to dream about having a large family.

Later, as I was single parenting two girls, then blending families and adding a third daughter, it still did not seem likely that we would ever become a large family. My vision and prayers for future generations were limited because of my current situation, but God was faithful to give visions to the next generation as was spoken by the prophet Joel and repeated later in Acts: "In the last days, God says, I will pour out my Spirit on all people. Your sons and daughters will prophesy, your young men will see visions, your old men will dream dreams" (Acts 2:17).

So it has been with our daughters. My first daughter, Katie, and her husband, Josh, both felt from their early dating years that God gave them the number of seven children for their family. They continued to pray about their family size with the addition of each child, knowing the costs and listening to cautious counsel from me. Pregnancy was very difficult for Katie physically, so I was anxious for my own baby's health. After their sixth child was a few years old and they had been praying about whether to have number seven, Katie told me one of her prayers was that I would also be excited about her having another pregnancy. She believes that prayer was answered because she excitedly took her pregnancy test in front of me while we were together at a family birthday celebration. My limited and cautious prayers were answered by an abundant God through the vision of the next generation.

There are many times when our adult children will have visions different from ours, but when we know they hear from God, it is easy to embrace and see His answers as "more than all we ask or imagine." With our first two daughters married, we have eleven grandchildren so far. It is a blessing I never dreamed of or prayed for, but God provided.

Are your prayers limited because of current circumstances or an inability to vision the future? Pray for your children and your children's children to hear from God and receive vision from Him. Sometimes praying the blessing Moses and Aaron spoke over the Israelites is a simple way for me to pray bigger vision for my family members:

> The LORD bless you
>   and keep you;
> the LORD make his face shine on you
>   and be gracious to you;
> the LORD turn his face toward you
>   and give you peace. (Numbers 6:24–26)

Receiving More in What Seems Impossible

We won't always experience abundant answers to prayers exactly as we prayed, but we'll receive more joy when we see how God makes things that seemed impossible come to fruition.

One seemingly impossible situation involved my mother's later years of life. My sweet mother, caring for an invalid husband over eight years, would often say, "There are many people worse off than we are." I wanted to correct her and remind her that her struggles and pain were pretty high on the list of suffering, from my perspective. But her humble heart and ability to look at others who were less fortunate kept her from becoming embittered or angry. She had chosen a marriage vow of "in sickness and in health" and lived that beautifully, even while other friends around her were traveling the world and living the retirement dream. Mom and Dad may not have ever enjoyed the world's pleasures, but she was joyful in all circumstances and managed to live on her limited income.

After Dad died, she took some years to pay off all the medical debt, and then she was able to travel with some church seniors' groups. Mother cared for family members and neighbors, full of joy in the hard times and in the good times. Although there were months I could not see a way out of her debt or a way she could live abundantly, God provided a full life even with her limited income. He continually provided more in what seemed like an impossible ask.

Another time I received more in what seemed impossible goes back to my prayers as a young believer, a girl of sixteen who dreamed of the foreign mission field. One of my earliest heroes of the faith was Elisabeth Elliot. I remember reading her book *Through Gates of Splendor* as a teenager and being enthralled with her life as she served alongside her husband, Jim Elliot, in Ecuador. Even after Jim was killed, Elisabeth continued to serve in that country and eventually witnessed to the tribe who had taken his life. I also remember reading her story and thinking that one of us was not like the other. While I yearned to serve on the foreign mission field, I was not going to attend Wheaton College and I didn't have the encouragement of anyone in my life to go into missions. My prayers instead became focused on other ways I could serve God in everyday life, since the mission field seemed too impossible to ask or imagine.

Fast-forward several decades to when I became a pastor of women's ministry, and my leaders *encouraged me* to go on mission trips and take teams of women. Over the next years, I was able to serve in Panama, Sri Lanka, Togo, and Nicaragua. Those mission trips have supplied me with friendships, teachings, and a renewed faith every time.

When I visited Sri Lanka, I witnessed women rising at four o'clock in the morning to have their time with God, prepare for their households, and then go to work to support their families. In addition, they served at their church every Saturday by visiting homes and then attended a Bible study one night a week. When telling us about their week, there was never complaining or whining about their long days and frequent nights at the church. The joy they mentioned from visiting homes and inviting people into their church community was greater than any sacrifice on their part.

Observing them causes me to serve more strongly and humbly. The women in villages of Nicaragua opened their front porches for home church meetings and often showed up with care packages for people in the local hospitals. The Nicaraguan women worship during services with their whole bodies, despite high temperatures and a lack of air-conditioning. Learning from women who serve their families and God in the most selfless ways has taught me about receiving more than just physical provision but also the abundant joy that is found in serving Him.

Their joy is abundant because of their uninhibited love for God, not because of provision. Women in Togo sometimes walk two miles each way to work, or they will share a moped with children strapped on their back. Those who have been blessed with a home open it up to also house widows and orphans. All of this is done because they love Jesus. They serve in a land of "the big God," and I believe because they see God as bigger, their joy is more abundant than mine. I went to serve and instead learned about joy. My teenage prayers to serve on a mission field were answered with more than I could ask or imagine.

ASK in Your Life

1. Where in your life do you have a great need right now and need "a big God," as Pastor Francis Avoyi described (page 42)? Meditate on Ephesians 1:19–20 to expand your vision of God.

2. How have your prayers been limited because of your current circumstances? Try praying some prayers from the Bible to expand yours. The blessing in Numbers 6:24–26 is a general blessing for current and future generations. 1 Samuel 1:27–28 is another passage to pray over your children. Pray for your family members by inserting their names into these passages.

3. If you've been on an international mission, have you noticed people in impoverished countries serving a big God with joy? If you're unable to go on a mission, read more about life in an under-resourced country. As a stretch goal, consider partnering with someone currently on a mission or who's going on a trip by supporting them financially or in prayer.

CHAPTER 4

ASK AS A BEGGAR

Sometimes we are not hungry enough in our prayers. Matthew Henry, in his commentary on Matthew 7:7, says the following about asking God in prayer:

> "*Ask*, as a beggar asks alms." Those that would be rich in grace, must betake themselves to the poor trade of begging, and they shall find it a thriving trade. "*Ask*; represent your wants and burdens to God, and refer yourselves to him for support and supply, according to his promise."[8]

When I think of a beggar, my mind goes to *Les Misérables* and the story of Jean Valjean, who spent nineteen years in jail and in the galleys (pulling ropes on a ship propelled only by men's arms) for stealing a loaf of bread. Most of us don't experience that kind of hunger for food in twenty-first-century America, but I can imagine the desperation that would lead someone to be a beggar. Without physical provision, without means to get provision, without hope.

When I first applied the Matthew 7:7 principle, I was certainly a beggar. I was at the bottom of an avalanche with only one way up. Maybe that was the secret sauce that made my first prayer with ASK so visibly successful. I had no ideas or solutions that seemed worthy, or I would have already done them. I was a person of action and had been getting things done since about the age of twelve. Today's world would have labeled me as an achiever, but my parents just called me a precocious firstborn leader. But in my first endeavor to ASK, I didn't have an action plan for even one of the four areas of my life that were busted. I simply prayed to God as a beggar.

Prayers without Answers

Another time I asked like a beggar—without answers, without a path, but desperate for answers—was when my sweet mother exhibited symptoms that she could no longer live alone. Midway into her seventies, she started a regimen of prescription meds and oxygen at night to help with her heart and lung issues. We thought she was managing these well until she started showing up for doctor's appointments on the wrong day or at church on a Saturday instead of Sunday morning.

Then one day a neighbor found Mother sitting on her front step in the ninety-degree heat, confused about how she got across the street. When I received the frantic call that this neighbor had called 911, I drove the three-hour trip in record time. The admitting doctor found that Mother had not been taking her heart medications in the right order, causing dementia. He kindly but sternly told me that she could not live alone any longer.

I packed Mother's suitcase and told her she would be coming to visit me for a few weeks while she recovered. Our house was not set up to accommodate senior care, with bedrooms upstairs, but my husband and I adapted for the short term and prayed about the long-term solution for my precious mother. She loved her home in Charlotte: her deck, her gardens, her church, and her friends of seventy-plus years.

But I had already spent many hours and days on the interstate going back and forth to check on her and knew that could not continue while I worked full-time. We had investigated senior-living options in Charlotte, and the costs of care were higher than in the low country of South Carolina. She was also on a fixed income with no retirement savings, so her possibilities were limited. I had no idea how we were going to provide the type of care she needed—and deserved. My prayers when I fell into the bed at night resembled that of Jean Valjean, begging God to hear me in my need. And though I had no plans to steal to make a pleasant home for her, the lack of money was our biggest obstacle. Watching and talking to many friends who were also in this season of caring for aging parents, my prayers were simply, "God, show us a way. Show her a way. Help us, God. Help."

After a month on consistent medications, the dementia diminished, and Mother was fully aware every day. One morning she came downstairs smiling, with a spring in her step and song in her voice as she said, "I've lived half my life in North Carolina. I think I'll live the rest of it here in South Carolina."

Astonished at her change of heart, I said, "Well, let's ask God where it will be best for you to live." That very day I noticed an ad in the newspaper with a special at a senior independent and assisted living home just seven minutes from our house. We went to see it, and Mother loved the rooms, the people, and the activities. Her long-term care insurance would pay the monthly rental amount for about thirty-six months. We moved Mother in, and she thrived there, being close to us and the great-grandchildren who came regularly to visit. I will admit to wondering how we would work out the finances after the thirty-six months were up, but Mother went to heaven in the thirty-fourth month.

God heard the cries of this beggar daughter and answered my prayers in a most beautiful way.

Prayers of Desperation

Although my praying as a beggar was for very different circumstances, the implication of begging God for an answer reminds me of the unique prayer of Hannah in 1 Samuel.

Not only had Hannah been barren for many years, but her rival wife, Peninnah, had sons and daughters. (Hannah's husband, Elkanah, had two wives.) Even though Hannah was barren, whenever Elkanah gave gifts to Peninnah and her children, he would give a double portion to Hannah because he loved her. Yet the Scriptures tell us that Peninnah taunted and provoked Hannah year after year. This is a story that could have been scripted in any middle school where mean girls are tormenting someone because of jealousy. This story of desperation tells us that Hannah wept and would not eat. On one of her annual visits to the tabernacle of the Lord, Hannah prayed and wept bitterly. Her grieving caused Hannah to make this vow as she prayed: "O Lord of Heaven's Armies, if you will look upon my sorrow and answer my prayer and give me a son, then I will give him back to you. He will be yours for his entire lifetime, and as a sign that he has been dedicated to the Lord, his hair will never be cut" (1:11 NLT).

The unique thing about Hannah's prayer is that in her position as a beggar, she attached a promise to the prayer. We've probably all attached a promise to a prayer, especially when desperate like Hannah. It might have even bordered on bargaining with God. In the midst of a crisis or praying for someone we love, we are prone to try to bargain. Maybe the promise went like this: "If you'll just do this, God, I will _____." You can fill in the blank: straighten up, eat healthier, quit drinking, stop swearing, read the Bible every day. But there are two unique attributes to Hannah's prayer that do not put it in the category of bargaining. First, Hannah did not offer to change her ways or habits, because she already believed and served God with all her heart. Second, she didn't just offer God a portion of her child—she promised Him the child's entire life would be spent in service to Him.

To pray as a beggar in desperation requires a surrendered heart and the resolve to continue serving God.

How many of us who are childless and praying would offer the child back for their lifetime? As compelling as this promise is, I don't think it was the conditions of Hannah's promise that caused God to respond but the surrender of her heart. God answered her prayer, and Hannah made good on the promise, giving her son, Samuel, back to Eli at the tabernacle after he had been weaned: "Oh, my lord! As you live, my lord, I am the woman who was standing here in your presence, praying to the LORD. For this child I prayed, and the LORD has granted me my petition that I made to him. Therefore I have lent him to the LORD. As long as he lives, he is lent to the LORD" (vv. 26–28 ESV). Even when life might have caused her to feel alone and abandoned by God, Hannah's beggar prayers show us a woman fully committed to Him. To pray as a beggar in desperation requires a surrendered heart and the resolve to continue serving God.

Turning Pain into Purpose

As we grow in our faith, we find that surrendering the outcome to a God we trust sometimes gives greater rewards than an immediate answer to our specific prayers. Looking back at the beggar Jean Valjean in *Les Misérables*, we can learn from this story even though it's fictional. Because he was once a beggar and understood desperate need, all of his later years were spent being generous. Once we have experienced emptiness in any form, that embedded memory can work for good to keep us focused more on the needs of others than ourselves.

This was certainly true for me. The years before I conceived, I remember desperately crying out to God for a child. Those years of seemingly unanswered prayers now give me compassion for those struggling with infertility. My years struggling as a single mom help me to be empathetic to the overwhelming needs of women in that same situation. Memories of those years are strong and come to mind when I see a single mom juggling childcare and her career, or childcare and serving in the church. Although I asked God many times during those eight years to bring me a husband and life partner, the pain of those years has now led me to find purpose by starting a ministry for single moms. My time spent caring for aging parents and desperately asking God for next steps keeps me tender to the needs of seniors and their children now caring for them.

What painful experience in your life or yet-to-be-answered prayer might God be using? What if the answers to our prayers, especially when we pray like beggars, has less to do with receiving the thing we prayed for and more to do with turning our pain into purpose? Can we trust Him for a bigger picture that He is working out things for our good?

Our experiences are never wasted if we use them for good. This is the understanding I have of the passage where Paul writes, "And we know that for those who love God all things work together for good, for those who are called according to his purpose" (Romans 8:28 ESV).

My friend and mentor Phyllis Lovelace Briscoe has translated this to me as "God doesn't waste a thing," and for that I am truly grateful.

ASK in Your Life

1. When have you prayed like Hannah, begging God for something in desperation? If your prayer of desperation leaned toward bargaining (or if you can imagine being in a situation like that), how could you have turned your bargaining into surrender?

2. Although it's difficult for us to imagine having a surrendered heart like Hannah's, in what area of your life does God want you to release your expectations and become aligned with Him?

3. What painful experience in your past or present might God want to turn into a purpose? What small step can you take this week to move forward toward fulfilling that purpose?

CHAPTER 5

ASK FOR A FRIEND, WITH A FRIEND

Most of my asks, seeks, and knocks have been for things I needed from God or for His direction in my life. But when you become a person of prayer, it's a natural progression to want to pray for others and talk to God about your friends and loved ones. This is called *intercession* and could easily be a book instead of just one chapter.

When it comes to asking for a friend, many times the request will be about a health issue. The Gospels demonstrate this when Jesus was traveling with the disciples and was continually approached by people who brought loved ones who needed healing to Him: "Now when the sun was setting, all those who had any who were sick with various diseases brought them to him, and he laid his hands on every one of them and healed them" (Luke 4:40 ESV).

When I pray for friends or loved ones, my theology is simple. If they are believers and want me to join them in prayer for themselves or a loved one, I think about the verse following the 7:7 principle in Matthew 7:9: "Which one of you, if his son asks him for bread, will give him a stone?" (ESV). When my friend who is asking for prayer is a son or daughter of the Father, I believe He wants to give them bread if they are asking for bread. We know that heaven—and eternity—is the goal and destination. But God also knows that from our limited human viewpoint, we want all who are sick to be healed, and we certainly desire for our loved ones to live a full life here on earth. So I partner with them in praying for their ask.

If the person asking is not a believer, then it's a great opportunity to share salvation with them. We know from watching Jesus interact with people that He was more concerned about the condition of their heart than with their health. Consider the case of when He healed a man who was paralyzed:

> And behold, some people brought to him a paralytic, lying on a bed. And when Jesus saw their faith, he said to the paralytic, "Take heart, my son; your sins are forgiven." And behold, some of the scribes said to themselves, "This man is blaspheming." But Jesus, knowing their thoughts, said, "Why do you think evil in your hearts? For which is easier, to say, 'Your sins are forgiven,' or to say, 'Rise and walk'? But that you may know that the Son of Man has authority on earth to forgive sins"—he then said to the paralytic—"Rise, pick up your bed and go home." (Matthew 9:2–6 ESV)

Or another healing was with the woman who had been bleeding for twelve years. She touched the hem of His garment, and "Jesus turned, and seeing her he said, 'Take heart, daughter; your faith has made you well'" (Matthew 9:22 ESV).

If the person's faith is evident, we can pray confidently for their ask. Sometimes, though, we find ourselves praying for a friend or loved one who is unable to ask for themselves, and we are unsure about their salvation. My first big ASK on this level came about ten years after my initial entry into my personal ASK journey. But before I get to the ask, let's look at how God prepared me for this journey into intercession. (I have a friend who calls Him "Jehovah-sneaky," and this story definitely has a setup orchestrated by God.)

The God Setup

Some women from our church in Charlotte attended a citywide prayer teaching by Anne Graham Lotz, the daughter of Billy Graham. Anne was teaching about the power of praying together and taught about triad praying—praying with three people—because of the Scripture that says, "A triple-braided cord is not easily broken" (Ecclesiastes 4:12 NLT).

She challenged us to separate into triads and agree to pray over the people each of us was praying on behalf of for salvation. One of my three names was my sister Barbara, so I wrote her name on the triad prayer list. Together with my new friends Kelly and Pat, we committed to pray over our list of nine names. We were new to the technology of three-way calling, where all of us could connect on the phone by pressing a few buttons. We agreed this would be the most consistent way for us to pray together weekly, given the demands of our full-time jobs and families. So for two months we called and connected for thirty minutes of prayer, sharing anything we saw God doing in the lives of the people on our list.

Two months into our triad praying, my sister Barbara, then thirty-eight, became sick with pneumonia. They airlifted her to a Charlotte hospital and diagnosed her with adult respiratory distress syndrome (ARDS). The doctors put her into a coma while on a ventilator to give her lungs a chance to heal. The prognosis was so grim that they didn't expect her to survive that first weekend.

Our family took shifts in the ICU waiting room. Since Barbara was on our triad's prayer list, I called my prayer partners, and we agreed to storm heaven for her body as well as her spirit. For twenty-one days, we prayed. My triad partners first called me on one of those long nights with a reference to the passage in Matthew 9 about the man who was paralyzed. Kelly said, "Jesus saw the faith of the friends who lowered the paralytic through the roof and then He healed the man. I believe our faith and our prayers are for this time, to pray for your sister."

For the next few weeks, Pat and Kelly continued to call and pray with me while I was in the waiting room, keeping watch and visiting Barbara for the allowed ten minutes every three hours. We enlisted our church and over seventy-five other churches across the southeast to pray. The emails and cards they sent with their prayers became a type of ASK note card as we posted each one on the glass walls of her ICU room. Nurses and other hospital staff would pause to read the prayers of strangers who didn't know Barbara but knew someone who had asked them to pray for her healing. Those believing prayers, as they were posted on the walls, might have made a greater impact than a note card with "Ask, Seek, and Knock" written on it because each one was a personal prayer.

I wasn't sure of Barbara's salvation and whether I should read Scripture over her, unsure of whether she could hear us while in her coma. Thankfully, a pastor friend visited her one day, and I explained my dilemma. He said, "Debbie, it's not whether she recognizes the words—it's the power of God's Word read over her. The nurses have said that many times patients hear words spoken to them while they are in a coma. So it's not about her familiarity with the Scriptures but our faith in believing them as we speak the words to her, much like a prayer spoken aloud in her presence." After that I read entire psalms and passages over her while combing her hair or massaging her hands. Even though the doctors were not hopeful or encouraging, after three weeks of touch-and-go survival, Barbara had improved enough to be taken off the ventilator.

Barbara didn't remember anything about her weeks in a coma, but she was astounded at the number of churches and people praying for her. After more weeks of recovery and physical therapy, she went to visit many of those churches who prayed for her healing. While her intention was to thank them and show them God's handiwork, I can only imagine how those visits must have encouraged the strangers who had been praying for a young woman they only knew by name.

After that illness, I talked to Barbara about Jesus on many occasions. I had kept a journal of those triad prayers that went up for her during the weeks in ICU. After reading the journal, Barbara told me that she believed in God and prayed to Him regularly. This gave me comfort years later, because she endured several other major health challenges over the next twenty years. Barbara finally succumbed to one of those challenges and passed to heaven. As I continue to grieve her loss, I'm comforted by imagining some of those prayer warriors who were already in heaven to greet her.

Sometimes when we ASK for someone else, it feels messy because we can't see everything God is doing in their heart.

Sometimes when we ASK for a family member or friend, it feels messy because we can't see everything God is doing in their hearts or lives. The ASK process then becomes more internal to our faith walk than to specific answers we can see to our prayers. We learn to trust God for the bigger picture and just ask, even when we cannot see the outcome.

Tuesday at 10

Another time I saw God do amazing things when "two or three are gathered in my name" (Matthew 18:19–20 ESV) was in my corporate setting. The global engineering company I used to work for had rehired me during my initial practice of the Matthew 7:7 principle (when I prayed for my house, job, body, and car), and I was now a few years into leading a team of fifteen administrative employees. One team member was a twenty-eight-year-old man I will call Tim, who had exhibited symptoms of liver failure. Tim had taken steroids while on his wrestling team in high school, and those drugs had done permanent damage to his liver. A few coworkers and I gathered in my office to pray for Tim, until the rest of the administrative team found out and wanted to join in.

This was in the nineties, and let me repeat—it was an engineering firm. This was way before creative work arrangements, work sharing, or flex time. We had strict office hours from 8:30 a.m. to 5:00 p.m. and were only allowed two ten-minute breaks per day, plus a lunch break. I was caught in a bind. I didn't want to leave people out of this praying circle, but I also didn't want to lose my job. So as our numbers grew, I went to our VP and asked permission for us to gather in my office—during our ten-minute break—once a week to pray for Tim. Our VP was a good-willed man and agreed to the request.

We called it our "Tuesday at 10" prayer gathering, and we spent most of our time praying for a new liver for Tim. Tim's family was grateful for the prayers and started communicating updates to us. He received the liver, and we all praised God for the outcome. When we visited Tim, he was amazed that his office team had been praying for him, but as a believer, he was excited about being used as the reason for our gathering.

He returned to work for a period, but a few years later he was struck with cancer, caused by the antirejection meds. We rallied again to pray for Tim, but this time he was not healed on earth. We were shocked and did not understand what God was doing. How could other asks we were praying for be answered when this whole group had begun for the purpose of praying for Tim? But then I remembered how God had worked within this group in so many other ways. We saw God do some miraculous things that we didn't even ask for. Several people in the prayer circle admitted to not knowing or trusting God and came to a believing knowledge of Jesus. A few started attending church or going back to churches they'd left in adulthood. Marriages were healed and children were restored to broken families.

I was asked by his family to speak at Tim's funeral, and with many tears I spoke about all the good that had come from Tim's earthly struggle. We had thought we were praying for one thing, one person, but God had a bigger picture in mind. I was truly humbled in thinking my initial Matthew 7:7 experiment had resulted in me being part of this workplace, where God had plans for my coworkers. I thought

He was providing me with employment that would provide financially for my family, but He was allowing me to be in a position to apply what I had learned from ask, seek, and knock for a greater purpose.

When we ask for a friend, sometimes we only see what is happening in the physical realm, not in the spiritual realm or from the eternal perspective of God. When we ask with a friend, we partner with others who might have their faith increased or bring needs of their own to prayer. Our ASKs become larger than what we, as one person, might put on a note card. Joining with and for others in prayer is a holy moment and expands God's kingdom as we link our hands and hearts together in one accord.

ASK in Your Life

1. What prayers do you have for someone else's need? How is intercession different from following the ask, seek, and knock steps for a personal need?

2. When have you experienced the power of praying together with two or more people? How was it different from praying alone?

3. If you haven't experienced the power of praying with others, who might you partner with now or in the future?

4. What prayer have you been praying that might have a greater purpose? Remember the example of the office group that prayed for a coworker's illness but also saw salvations and healed marriages as a result. If you've experienced something like this, write it down and share it with someone as an exercise in growing a deeper understanding of prayer.

PART TWO

SEEK

CHAPTER 6

SEEK AND FIND

When we read the word *seek*, "see" jumps right out at us, which suggests using our eyes. But the Greek word for "seek" really pushes us past "see" to look toward a more demanding inquiry, according to *Strong's Concordance*: "to seek by *inquiring*, to investigate to reach a *binding* (terminal) resolution; to search, 'getting to the bottom of a matter.'"[9]

Many times our prayers are cries without any answer in sight, just crying out while we ask God to provide solutions. That was certainly the initial stage of my Matthew 7:7 ASK when I was crying out "house—job—body—car" and feeling stuck in those four areas. After the initial ask, even in my childlike approach, I knew that some work was required on my part. Thus began the *seek* part of this equation. In the ASK prayer process, the step of *seeking* means actively looking for solutions or answers to your prayer. I didn't know at first that the Greek meaning of "seek" was "getting to the bottom of a matter," but I knew that God created me with a mind and abilities to think and reason. I knew He expected me to use that mind instead of just sitting with open hands waiting for gifts to fall from heaven.

Now this is where it does get tricky. I can certainly make some things happen in my own strength, and I'm sure some of you can too. There's a tension involved in employing our abilities while listening to God during the seek step that gets refined with practice. Maybe you are new to the Matthew 7:7 journey and want some guardrails to help you learn how to seek without taking control of every situation.

As someone who also has the proclivity to be over-responsible, I've only learned to manage this through time and experience. At times I will make a pros and cons list, and because I think in Excel spreadsheets, you'd better believe I have a template for those lists. Using lists and then sorting the options utilizes the very abilities God gave me, so I can't imagine He doesn't want me to use those tools. Where I can take this too far in prayer, though, is to rely solely on the lists. It's tempting to sort through all the logistics of a decision, pray about it, and then before God answers make the decision based on my own logic. We can certainly do this—and often be successful in our efforts—but we lose the strength of knowing that God was leading us. We also might miss the beauty of what other things He had in store had we surrendered the decision to Him in prayer.

A pros and cons list can help guide me in making a life decision or major purchase, but if I'm praying about this decision as an ASK to God, there are intrinsic costs and benefits that won't be captured on a spreadsheet. Some questions I might take to God during the *seek* portion of an ASK are:

- Will this purchase or decision honor God?
- Will it cost me time, energy, or focus better spent on kingdom priorities?
- Is it the right time to make this decision? Or does God have more for me if I wait?

These types of questions can't be quantified with an easy yes or no on a pros and cons list. Instead, they involve the spiritual discernment we will explore in this "Seek" part of the book.

One analogy that has helped me in the seek portion of my ASKs is jigsaw puzzles. I love puzzles and have learned to work on them to unwind and relax, putting my mind to work on those pieces and letting the other parts of my brain take a rest. Some things true about piecing jigsaw puzzles together also apply in how we seek God on an ask:

1. My puzzle working starts with the outer edges, and then I sort according to color and shape. With an ask, I have to sort out obvious paths and eliminate ones that I know are not best. This is where writing down possible solutions is helpful because you can check each one against Scripture, making sure it lines up with God's best for you. Through the following chapters, you will see that ASK prayer isn't always transactional. There will be some prayers when the solution feels out of your control, but God will be actively working to align your will with His.

2. You can't force the pieces. If you do, it will cause rework. Same with our asks. If there's no obvious solution, waiting can sometimes be your best action. For example, maybe you are praying for a new manager to replace your current one who is difficult to work with. If you force a solution that will meet your needs and leave for a new job, you may miss something God wanted to do with the current working relationship.

3. Sometimes the next piece isn't obvious, and it's easy to get stuck. My daughter Caroline taught me to move past the stuck places of my jigsaw puzzles and come back to them later. Remember that part of the ASK prayer exercise is releasing the area to God for His wisdom and direction. If we pray with a step or solution in mind but are stuck without seeing a way forward, we might be trying to control the answer.

4. I can't work puzzles in the dark. No matter how many extra lamps I use, I've found it best to work in the daylight. Likewise with seeking and finding the answer to our ask. If we hold up the answers to God, talk to Him humbly and honestly, and ask

Him to illuminate any dark places or sinful longings, it will help to confirm if an answer is from Him or if self is taking over.

Using those principles, here's an example of a time when I was seeking God's answers regarding a big decision for our family.

Working a Life Puzzle

When Gibson and I were dating he was working on a field assignment in Richmond, Virginia, and the girls and I were in Charlotte. There were a lot of weekend travels, emails, and phone calls to keep us connected, until the long distance became too much. Gibson proposed to me one May evening after a family wedding we all attended. One of the first things we did was pray that God would guide us in the future months to make plans and align our desire to get married with our work and home and family needs. Then he approached the engineering company and asked for a transfer back to Charlotte, which they approved for the following April. We set our wedding date for that month and began making plans. Since I was renting a house with the girls, we started looking for a house to purchase but knew that summer was too early to buy if we weren't getting married until the next spring. *(Start with the outer edge and sort the colors.)*

One day my thirteen-year-old, Katie, was out riding her bicycle in the neighborhood. She flew through the door screaming, "It's for sale! It's for sale!" After she calmed down, she told me that our dream house had a FOR SALE sign in the yard. The girls and I drove past this house every time I took them to school. When you are a single mama and have rented and moved four times in five years, it's easy to dream about the stability of a brick house with green grass and lots of windows to decorate at Christmas. This house had a sweeping staircase, and I imagined mums on every step in the fall and poinsettias at Christmas. Although my heart leapt at the fact that this house was on the market, I reminded Katie that Gibson and I weren't getting married for another eight to nine months, and there was no way I could purchase a house on my salary alone. Trying to purchase the house alone, for either me or Gibson, was not the dream. It needed to work for our new family or we would be forcing a solution that didn't fit. *(Don't force the pieces.)*

In a childlike ask, Katie encouraged us to just go look at the house the next weekend when Gibson came to visit. It didn't hurt that Katie's best friend's father was the listing real estate agent, and she had already told him we wanted to see it while hanging out at their house. I had been living the past ten years in a poverty mentality. Nothing about this house scenario made sense to me financially or timing-wise. It seemed there was no way to move forward, but I submitted to the Lord and my future husband to see what they thought about it. Sometimes even when answers are developing before our eyes, we ignore them or bypass a God-solution because of our wounded pasts or an unhealthy mindset. It's important to remember that God holds solutions to every puzzle and that we need to keep an open viewpoint about possible answers to push past any roadblocks. *(Don't get stuck.)*

Gibson and I went to see the house, and it was beyond all our hopes and dreams. With every corner we turned, we smiled at how it checked all the boxes of our wish list. But then reality set in when the real estate agent told us that the owners had been transferred to California and were looking for a quick sale. With Gibson living six hours away until his relocation the next year, there was no way for us to purchase this house before someone else made an offer.

We went back to my rental house, and before even talking to the girls, we knelt down on the worn, nappy carpet and prayed. We were honest with God and told Him we had done the due diligence, run the numbers, and investigated the options, but we did not see a way to purchase this home. At the end, Gibson said the sweetest surrender prayer I've ever heard: "God, we just don't see a way to purchase this. If you want us to have this house, you are going to have to make it happen." Surrendering our inability to make it work in our own strength was an important step in denying our self-sufficiency. *(Hold everything up to the light.)*

The next day at church, a mutual friend approached Gibson and told him that he had a loss-prevention engineering job opening (the same as Gibson's current position) and would like him to interview for it. Gibson said, "You know I'm living in Richmond, Virginia, right now?" The friend said, "Yes, and we will pay for you to relocate back here to Charlotte as soon as next month."

We could never have imagined that God would arrange another job! He got the job, we made an offer on the house, Gibson moved back to Charlotte, and we moved our wedding date up seven months to November, when we began living in our dream house.

Nothing about purchasing that house seemed easy or in the right order, but the steps fell into place much like one of my thousand-piece puzzles. That house was the beginning of a hard first eight years of our marriage as a blended family. Although houses do not make families, I believe this answered prayer was certainly God's way of putting glue on all the broken pieces of the two families we were blending. Each one of us has such treasured memories of that dream home that on almost every trip back to Charlotte now—even many years after we moved away—one of us can be found parking in front of it to reminisce. We are not just remembering the windows lit up at Christmas but the trees when they got toilet-papered by teenage friends. We are not just remembering mums and poinsettias on the front steps but prom pictures and Easter photos. When I think about the memories we would've missed by not seeking God's best for our family and working the puzzle, it reinforces this part of the ASK equation that requires stepping through a crack in the door and trusting Him to swing it wide open.

Which part of the jigsaw puzzle analogy will most help you as you seek God's answers to your prayers? Are you overwhelmed thinking about your situation or a current dilemma and need to start by dreaming bigger or brainstorming possible next steps to line up the outer edges? Or maybe you are like me and decisions come easy when making a spreadsheet or pros and cons list, but perhaps God wants you to slow down to keep from forcing the pieces. Do you sometimes get stuck when praying about something because nothing seems to fit your definition of the right answer? Finally, although seeking is active, part of that activity means we filter every possible answer through God's Word and His best wisdom for us to know if we're seeing it in the light.

Write It in Neon on the Sidewalk

Many times in my prayer journey, the ASKs have been about small decisions when seeking God's best was not a life-altering moment. Although every decision seems large when it's looming in front of you, in the scheme of life, many are small. Occasionally, though, the ask will involve a major life change or impact my future or the future of others. It is for those ASKs that I sometimes need to use clarifying questions about the request while I am seeking. Maybe this step is just to remind my spirit about the importance of a specific prayer, or saying it aloud to God helps me remember not to move ahead without His confirmation, but it's still a needed addition.

Twenty-five years ago, whenever I had a major decision to make, my ask would be followed by, "God, when you answer me, will you write it in neon on the sidewalk?" I cannot remember if I heard this from another speaker or was crying out from my overwhelmed state. Other working mamas will agree that sometimes between school schedules, homework, and work demands, our prayer life on any given night is a deep sigh along with a "Help me, Lord" thrown in. Most of the time, life was happening at lightning speed, and there was a chance I might miss an answer from the most high God even if I was seeking and paying attention.

I've heard other people phrase this as asking God to put it on a billboard. For me, the sidewalk is in front of me whenever I'm walking, and neon is a color that will be noticed no matter how fast I'm going. I know that God doesn't want me to miss the things that will affect my life course, much like we earthly parents might not always stop our children when they are running too fast and might fall in the grass, but we're not going to let them run out in front of a car. So in asking for neon on the sidewalk, I'm essentially saying, "God, don't let me miss something You have for me."

"God, don't let me miss something You have for me."

One time this was helpful to me was when our daughter Jess and her husband, Nick, were moving their family to Charleston from Indiana. They asked us to help find rental homes in a specific neighborhood where Nick felt called to plant a church. This was an important move for them, and I knew finding a home was key to their relocation. I'd driven through the neighborhood with a girlfriend, and nothing was for rent. We had all looked through online options, but this was before apps showed properties almost as soon as they were available.

One night, my husband and I took another trip downtown, and I prayed, *Lord, please don't let us miss it; write it on the sidewalk in neon.* We again weren't seeing any "for rent" signs and were about to give up when Gibson spotted a small hand-printed sign stuck in a front window with a phone number to call. We looked through the windows and sent the information to Jess and Nick. The house not only turned out to be a great place for their family to live but was within walking distance of a building that would one day (six years later) house their church. Nick had prayer-walked around that building for years as he prayed about the church they were called to plant.

It wasn't neon and it wasn't on the sidewalk. But I think about that little sign in the window whenever I want to ask God to make sure I don't miss an important next step! If it's important to my future and I'm asking, He won't let me miss it.

Moses Didn't have Neon or Sidewalks

Moses didn't have neon paint or sidewalks, but his example continues to teach me about taking specific leading and instruction about next steps from God. There are times in reading about Moses and the Israelites' exodus from Egypt that I'm thankful not to have been born in that age. Numbers 9 is just one chapter that makes me glad to be a baby boomer. In this chapter, Moses had built the tabernacle according to God's specifications and was establishing law and order in the wilderness. These rules, ceremonies, and sanctifications were necessary because the Israelites had been such a rowdy and rebellious bunch. There were also over six hundred thousand of them traveling together, along with women and children who were not counted. So, some semblance of order and adherence to rules was definitely needed. The one guideline I'm sure would have been difficult for me as a pioneer and apostle to follow was waiting to move with the cloud of God's presence over the tabernacle:

> On the day the tabernacle, the tent of the covenant law, was set up, the cloud covered it. . . . Whenever the cloud lifted from above the tent, the Israelites set out; wherever the cloud settled, the Israelites encamped. At the LORD's command the Israelites set out, and at his command they encamped. As long as the cloud stayed over the tabernacle, they remained in camp. . . . Sometimes the cloud stayed only from evening till morning, and when it lifted in the morning, they set out. Whether by day or by night, whenever the cloud lifted, they set out. Whether the cloud stayed over the tabernacle for two days or a month or a year, the Israelites would remain in camp and not set out; but when it lifted, they would set out. At the LORD's command they encamped, and at the LORD's command they set out. They obeyed the LORD's order, in accordance with his command through Moses. (Numbers 9:15, 17–18, 21–23)

Do you see some of the nuances about this order from God? The cloud could have stayed over the tabernacle for two days or a month or a year, and the Israelites would stay put. That's some real obedience, don't you think? I can only imagine people getting a little stir-crazy after months in one location, especially with close to a million people and animals in the same camp! And sometimes the cloud would only stay from evening until morning, when they had to set out again. I admit that I would be one of the wives sinfully complaining because the bags were just unpacked and it was time to pack them again.

Perhaps Moses was thinking about all these variables when he asked God to lead them out of the wilderness. In Exodus, we hear just how Moses was pleading with God for guidance:

> Moses said to the LORD, "You have been telling me, 'Lead these people,' but you have not let me know whom you will send with me. You have said, 'I know you by name and you have found favor with me.' If you are pleased with me, teach me your ways so I may know you and continue to find favor with you. Remember that this nation is your people."
>
> The LORD replied, "My Presence will go with you, and I will give you rest." (33:12–14)

If you have a big ask and want to make sure you don't miss God's leading, be bold like Moses and ask Him for a cloud. Or if you need something more obvious, like I do, maybe ask for neon on the sidewalk. Then seek His answer and get to the bottom of the matter.

ASK in Your Life

1. How might you seek in a current ASK by actively looking for solutions or answers to your prayer?

2. Which of the questions on page 68 might help you in discerning next steps in the ASK?

3. Using the puzzle analogy, where might you be forcing the pieces or getting stuck in a current prayer? How can you shine the light on this need to help with moving forward?

4. What past wound or unhealthy mindset (like the one mentioned on page 71) is keeping you stuck in a situation? Who is a good friend or accountability person who can help you seek in this ASK?

5. If you need more biblical inspiration about seeking God for next steps, read Numbers 9:15–23 and take note of how many times Moses waited for God's presence before taking a step.

CHAPTER 7

SEEK AND LISTEN

Sometimes seeking God in prayer requires us to use two of our primary tools for communicating: listening and speaking. Even if you've heard the biblical account of Samuel and Eli before, it's a powerful lesson for all of us on hearing from God.

> The boy Samuel ministered before the LORD under Eli. In those days the word of the LORD was rare; there were not many visions.
>
> One night Eli, whose eyes were becoming so weak that he could barely see, was lying down in his usual place. The lamp of God had not yet gone out, and Samuel was lying down in the house of the LORD, where the ark of God was. Then the LORD called Samuel.
>
> Samuel answered, "Here I am." And he ran to Eli and said, "Here I am; you called me."
>
> But Eli said, "I did not call; go back and lie down." So he went and lay down.
>
> Again the LORD called, "Samuel!" And Samuel got up and went to Eli and said, "Here I am; you called me."
>
> "My son," Eli said, "I did not call; go back and lie down."

Now Samuel did not yet know the LORD: The word of the LORD had not yet been revealed to him.

A third time the LORD called, "Samuel!" And Samuel got up and went to Eli and said, "Here I am; you called me."

Then Eli realized that the LORD was calling the boy. So Eli told Samuel, "Go and lie down, and if he calls you, say, 'Speak, LORD, for your servant is listening.'" So Samuel went and lay down in his place.

The LORD came and stood there, calling as at the other times, "Samuel! Samuel!"

Then Samuel said, "Speak, for your servant is listening."

And the LORD said to Samuel: "See, I am about to do something in Israel that will make the ears of everyone who hears about it tingle." (1 Samuel 3:1–11)

Just imagine if Eli did not recognize the voice of God and missed the opportunity to teach Samuel the most valuable lesson of his life. Just imagine if, when Samuel came to Eli a third time, Eli had gotten frustrated and yelled at Samuel to quit waking him up. What if Eli had not paused long enough to realize that the voice of God was speaking to Samuel? Later in that same chapter we see just how life-changing that middle-of-the-night moment was: "The LORD was with Samuel as he grew up, and he let none of Samuel's words fall to the ground. And all Israel from Dan to Beersheba recognized that Samuel was attested as a prophet of the LORD. The LORD continued to appear at Shiloh, and there he revealed himself to Samuel through his word" (vv. 19–21).

Scholars say that Samuel was about eleven years old when he was serving with Eli and first heard God speak. I was about that same age when a woman taught me how to pray, and that moment was as life-changing for me as it was for Samuel.

I was helping Mrs. Terra Gaye Williams lead a boys' choir at our church and spent many afternoons at her house learning how to accompany her direction and practicing the piano music. One of those days, I remember Mrs. Williams kneeling with me at her coffee table to pray. Her small children were playing nearby. We didn't have our Bibles open, and we didn't recite any Scripture. She taught me to speak out loud to the Lord and tell Him what was on my heart. That was my first introduction to having a conversation with God.

Just as with our human conversations, we *talk* and we *listen*. Mrs. Williams showed me in a simple but powerful way how to talk to God and then how to listen for His answers. She demonstrated how she talked to God with questions about how to parent her children. Then she shared examples of parenting insights she heard as she listened to His voice in the wisdom of trusted friends in the days after she talked to God about that subject.

Her confidence instilled hope in me. If God spoke to her, I believed He would do the same for me. I did not hear God's voice that day, but I believe it was her example and that hope that allowed me to hear God's voice a few years later when I answered an altar call at a revival—and asked Jesus into my heart.

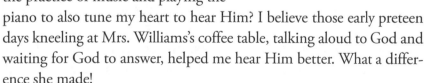

Are your conversations with God one-sided, or do you pause to give Him time to speak and answer?

Could it be that God was using the practice of music and playing the piano to also tune my heart to hear Him? I believe those early preteen days kneeling at Mrs. Williams's coffee table, talking aloud to God and waiting for God to answer, helped me hear Him better. What a difference she made!

Are your conversations with God one-sided, or do you pause to give Him time to speak and answer? Many times we are uncomfortable with silence, so we fill up the air with words and talking. I like to think of God as a best friend who knows me so well that He is willing to hear me ramble and repeat things without correction, but He also has something to say in return to my questions. Conversational prayer helps us sharpen our listening skills because we remember there are two voices in the dialogue.

Listening with a Tuned Ear

As we mature in our faith, we tune our listening for His voice to line up with what we know to be God's will. If you've ever been in an orchestra or watched one perform, there are a few minutes before the first song when all the instruments are tuned. Or sometimes in a band, guitar players will tune their strings before singing a song. Tuning an instrument is important because tuning ensures that the other instruments (voice or orchestra) are on the same pitch. It's important for us too when listening for God's voice to be tuned to His frequency.

A passage from Proverbs 2 talks about "making your ear attentive to wisdom," which is tuning our ear to God:

> My son, if you receive my words
> and treasure up my commandments with you,
> making your ear attentive to wisdom
> and inclining your heart to understanding;
> yes, if you call out for insight
> and raise your voice for understanding,
> if you seek it like silver
> and search for it as for hidden treasures,
> then you will understand the fear of the LORD
> and find the knowledge of God. (vv. 1–5 ESV)

Even though there are several occasions in the Bible when God's people audibly heard His voice, I believe we can each hear from God based on how we are individually and uniquely created. He knows us because He created us, as we remember from Psalm 139:

> For you created my inmost being;
> you knit me together in my mother's womb.
> I praise you because I am fearfully and wonderfully made;
> your works are wonderful,

I know that full well.
My frame was not hidden from you
    when I was made in the secret place,
    when I was woven together in the depths of the earth.
      (vv. 13–15)

For example, music has been a part of my life since I started playing the piano at age six, and I accompanied children's choirs by the age of twelve. In high school I sang in church choirs, and then in my twenties and thirties I sang in adult choirs, played bells, and was part of a singers' ensemble. There are many old hymns whose lyrics have reinforced God's Word to me over the years, and also several times I've felt God speaking through a specific phrase or chorus of a worship song. I've learned to pay attention to God speaking to me through songs.

One summer, our family changed churches. Even though we knew God had prompted us to go to another church, it was difficult to leave a congregation whose members were like family and where we had been serving and leading for over fifteen years. Gibson and I had been praying about a new church home as we visited several over the summer. By fall, we felt sure we had found the right one to meet the needs of our teenager, our toddler, and our blended family. Except it left a hole for me without a way to worship through music ministry. Leaving our singers' group behind was the hardest because the music inspired me week after week and the members were like brothers and sisters. Our new church had an established (and younger) praise team, not a choir or ensemble. But because it seemed like a good fit for our family, I prayed and asked God how to fill the gap.

From almost the second or third Sunday we visited, whenever I was feeling the loss of my old group, the praise team sang a song I had never heard before. The worshipful sway of the crowd and simple lyrics reminded me that perhaps I had made singing—I had made worship—about leading worship or being a part of a choir when all along the heart of worship is all about Jesus. It was as if God was singing those words over my soul, whispering a gentle answer to my ask. Through music, He was telling me that worship was more than a song. His prompting through the repeated lyrics caused me to keep my eyes open and seek an answer in a new place.

After I observed a new way to worship (without being in an ensemble), I began looking for other ways to serve in this new church of ours. Then, surrendering my former church identity and opening my heart of worship to new areas of serving, God showed me other ways to worship. This church had a ministry for working women, and I was asked to serve on the leadership board. Gibson and I also joined a blended families ministry that met every Sunday, and we were asked to mentor other newly married couples. God used a song to break my long-standing ways of worship and to show me other ways to worship Him.

Maybe worship or song lyrics aren't how God will speak to you in your seeking. Perhaps your ear is tuned to nature, and you hear His voice through the tides pounding on the beach or the sun setting behind a mountain range. Or it could be that your ear is tuned to words, and the written word will jump off the pages of a book or your Bible with God's voice.

Listening to Scripture

Fast-forward a few years after we changed churches to the beginning of yet another faith journey. This time God spoke to me in a different way. Gibson's job had ended after the 9/11 disaster, when most insurance companies were restructuring due to huge financial losses. His severance would end in just three months. The engineering company I worked for went through a merger, and my severance would also run out at the end of the year. There were a few scary months in there. My journal entries from that time show the raw fear and lack of trust for our provision.

My ASK was big but simple. One of us needed a full-time job in the next three months, and we were dependent on God to clearly give us next steps in our job searches. We had one daughter in out-of-state college, one graduating high school, and a five-year-old to support. The stakes were high. But upon closer examination, one thing other than fear showed up in my prayer times as I journaled through this season with God. He was speaking to me through a passage from Isaiah 40. Here are some of my journal entries:

10/27/01—Still feeling impatient, God. How much do I do vs wait on You to do? One of us needs a paycheck, preferably both. Waiting but not patiently.

10/28/01—Again! An email devotion on "moving in presumption" reminded me that You really want me to seek confirmation before next steps.

11/10/01—Read in my Woman of Purpose book this passage: Do you not know? Have you not heard? The LORD is the everlasting God, the Creator of the ends of the earth. He will not grow tired or weary, and his understanding no one can fathom. He gives strength to the weary and increases the power of the weak. Even youths grow tired and weary, and young men stumble and fall; but those who hope in the LORD will renew their strength. They will soar on wings like eagles; they will run and not grow weary, they will walk and not be faint. Isaiah 40:28–31 NIV

11/11/01—Sermon series is on Faith and Waiting and Pastor Chadwick preached from Isaiah 40:31. WAIT flashed on the screen. Then the worship song was "Wait on the Lord."

12/6/01—Gibson's interview with the Navy in Charleston, SC.

12/31/01—Gibson accepts job offer and we plan to relocate our family.

1/3/02—Awakened by the Lord at 4am, I turned to Is 40:31 to see if there was anything else HE wanted to teach me there. I felt that v 28 "to the ends of the earth" speaks to Charleston and the seas. Then turned in my Woman of Purpose study to the next section. It was a section about moving, a wife's calling and Isaiah 40:31. Attending a Bible study at another church this evening, the Pastor started a 3-part message of One Yoked Eagles (Is 40:31) and the service ended with a song about eagles.

Maybe you've moved your family many times for employment. For me, a woman who had been born and lived in the same city for over forty years, moving even four hours away from family felt like the ends of the earth. I desperately needed God to speak and answer this rooted woman's ASK—and He did.

God loves to speak to us through His Word, and it helps if we are familiar with it. Even when we're not, He will use Bible studies, sermons, and songs to bring a passage to our mind and then confirm the Scripture just as He did during my season of waiting with Isaiah 40:31. Sometimes we just need to tune our ears. Other times we have to tune our hearts to let His words be heard above the roar of our own selfish desires. I'm grateful that He pursues us and speaks when we seek Him in prayer, if we will just listen.

ASK in Your Life

1. How can you use Eli's example of guiding Samuel in conversational prayer to grow more patient in your own prayer life or in leading someone younger in prayer?
2. How does Proverbs 2:1–5 inspire you to tune your ear toward God and His wisdom?
3. How has God spoken to you through worship or Scripture or nature? In what other ways might your ear be tuned to God?
4. What are the benefits of regular Bible study or daily reading, as seen in the example of God speaking through Isaiah 40? How can you tune your heart to God just a little more in this way?

CHAPTER 8

SEEK AND OBSERVE

W hen we are praying, it is part of *seeking* to keep our eyes and ears open to what God is saying in various forms. In more recent years as I've used the ASK prayer challenge, there's a part of seeking where it's helpful to observe and take note. *Observe* is defined as "*to regard with attention*, especially so as to see or learn something."[10] While I am releasing all anxiety and worry about the ASK, it's important for me to still pay focused attention to see and learn. In prayer, observing requires me to watch, take note, and make a deeper inquiry into all possibilities. To help me in this part of the prayer journey, there are four steps I remember using the acronym SEEK: *search, explore, examine*, and *keep record*.

Search My Heart

The first thing I need to do when seeking God's best in prayer is to search my heart by asking more specific questions about my ASK. Hopefully I already did this when I first presented my need to God, but sometimes it's later in the process before I press in with more questions. There are two questions I try to ask here. The first is, Will having an answer to this help me fulfill God's purpose on earth? Whenever I am trying to answer this question, I go back to the Great Commission Jesus spoke over His disciples as a parting directive: "All authority in heaven and on earth has been given to me. Therefore go and make disciples of all nations, baptizing them in the name of the Father and of the Son and of the Holy Spirit, and teaching them to obey everything I have commanded you. And surely I am with you always, to the very end of the age" (Matthew 28:18–20). Is my heart being led to continue this work on earth, or am I distracted from it?

The second question I ask to root out any selfishly focused prayers of mine is, Will it bless others or just me? David cried out in Psalm 139 with similar questions:

> Search me, God, and know my heart;
>   test me and know my anxious thoughts.
> See if there is any offensive way in me,
>   and lead me in the way everlasting. (vv. 23–24)

As in David's example, sometimes the selfish desires of my heart are hidden even from me, but not from God. If I humbly come before God and ask Him to search my heart, He usually nudges me through a message or a devotion or a passage of Scripture I've read immediately following my ask.

It may be when I started my ASK, I was too close to the area or problem to objectively search my heart in the matter. Often when we are too close to a situation, it's difficult to ask ourselves the hard questions. After I've asked these questions, it's easier to press forward and pray over this ASK with confidence.

Explore All Scenarios

Journaling during a recent ASK exercise, some of my questions turned from examining my heart to exploring all scenarios or possible answers. Sometimes exploring all the options is as simple as asking, "What else, God?" If I'm not paying attention and observing everything around me related to an ASK, there may be creative solutions I miss or a pathway not taken. I have a pretty linear mind, so creativity does not come easily. Maybe you're wired differently and are able to vision and dream as you are doing laundry or preparing dinner. Because I'm pragmatic and function with routines and rhythms, there have been a few times when God had to interrupt my thinking and guide me in exploring all my options with a dream.

If I'm not paying attention and observing everything around me related to an ASK, there may be creative solutions I miss or a pathway not taken.

Explore a Dream

Some people in the Bible received prophetic dreams that revealed God's next steps for them. In the Old Testament, one of the most famous dreamers is Joseph. In Genesis 40, he interpreted dreams of Pharaoh's cupbearer and baker, which gave him street cred with Pharaoh. When Pharaoh later needed a dream interpreted, he asked for Joseph. God's purpose was to raise Joseph from prison to second-in-command over Egypt and to save the Egyptians and the Israelites from a horrible famine. The dream occurred, Joseph interpreted it, then the interpretation came to be.

One of the most eternity-impacting dreams came to another Joseph—in the New Testament. Joseph would have divorced his fiancée Mary when he found out she was pregnant, but God sent an angel to him in a dream, convincing him that the pregnancy was of God. Joseph went ahead with the marriage. After Jesus was born, God sent two more dreams, one to tell Joseph to take his family to Egypt so the evil king Herod could not kill Jesus and another to tell him Herod was dead and that he could return home.

When we explore our dreams, it's important to separate the fantastical or bad-pizza dreams from ones that might contain vision from God. I estimate that I remember dreams at least one night per week, so that equals almost twenty-six hundred dreams I've remembered since the age of sixteen. Out of that estimated twenty-six hundred, there have been less than a handful worth noting, exploring, and examining through the lens of Scripture. One in particular was timely and hopeful for me during a time when I was praying to God frequently about a repeated ASK.

Remarriage or Singleness?

A few years into my life as a single mom, I remember thinking, "This is not the life I planned or wanted." Being single presented an emptiness that felt unnatural. Even though these years were some of my sweetest times with the Lord, I maintained a deep longing to be married and have a life companion. Well-meaning friends arranged blind dates and singles ministries at my church introduced me to other men, but none seemed to fit the picture of who I knew God desired for my life. Also, it was difficult enough to work full-time, raise two children, and manage a home without also finding time to date. Finally, one day I had a long talk with God and told Him that I was done trying to make this happen on my own. While I didn't expect Him to drop my future husband on my doorstep, I needed to hear whether or not I was supposed to remarry.

I had explored Paul's writings on divorce, marriage, and singleness enough to quote him when praying: "Now to the unmarried and the widows I say: It is good for them to stay unmarried, as I do. But if they cannot control themselves, they should marry, for it is better to marry than to burn with passion" (1 Corinthians 7:8–9). That night after my long talk with God about burning with passion (really, I think I just said, "Either take away my desire or bring the man to meet the desire"), I had a dream. In this dream, I met a new engineer at my workplace, and then he was standing at my apartment door ringing the doorbell. He seemed youthful and handsome, and I had the strong sense that this was my future husband.

Having this dream proved a little tricky, because as a manager, I had a self-imposed rule about not dating any of the engineers in our company. I wasn't sure how God would work that part out, but I finally felt at peace about my desires and my future. I laid down my efforts to make a relationship happen through blind dates or extra events that took me away from the girls. I felt confident that God had someone in mind for me and that He would make it evident.

The next month at work, a new engineer started who was at least ten years younger than me and not at all attractive to me. I remember silently asking, "Is this him, God?" only to breathe a huge sigh of relief the next day when I found out he was engaged. I pushed aside the dream and went on with life, resting in the fact that no more striving was needed on my part to make it happen. The dream had released me from trying to work this out on my own, and I could move forward with peace and confidence in God's timing and leading.

During that same time, Gibson had also started to work at my company, but I didn't think he was the one from the dream because I was no longer searching. About nine months after he started to work there, Gibson asked me out on Valentine's Day. I told him the girls and I were busy making a hospital visit, but he could come over later for coffee. When he arrived at my apartment door that night and I looked through the peephole, I remembered the dream and that Gibson was the face in the dream. Of course, Gibson had not had any such dream, so it took him about two and half years to hear from God and propose marriage, but I was patient, believing he was the one God had chosen.

Examine in the Light

Once we've explored various options and scenarios (or even had one presented in a dream), it's important to examine them in the light. When I wake in the middle of the night, stumbling in the dark without benefit of glasses or contact lens, it's difficult to be sure of my steps. Likewise with possible pathways for us to follow regarding our ASKs, examining them in the light will keep us from stumbling. As followers of Jesus, we know this also prevents us from making wrong decisions or choosing options opposite of God's best for us: "For you were once darkness, but now you are light in the Lord. Live as children of light (for the fruit of the light consists in all goodness, righteousness and truth) and find out what pleases the Lord" (Ephesians 5:8–10).

So we examine and ask, "God, is this pathway one that pleases You?" Asking that simple question starts my conversation with Him, but asking if the solution lines up with God's perfect will is even more complex. As I am listening for His answers, I need to check those against Scripture to make sure the solution lines up with God's truth. For example, when I was praying about whether to remain single or one day consider remarriage, the answer God brought to me in a dream confirmed that remarriage was in my future. Did the answer of remarriage line up with God's will? In the Bible, starting in Genesis 2, we see that God created man and then created woman to be his companion. I had also explored what God told His people about divorce and what Jesus said when the Pharisees asked Him:

> "Why then," they asked, "did Moses command that a man give his wife a certificate of divorce and send her away?"
>
> Jesus replied, "Moses permitted you to divorce your wives because your hearts were hard. But it was not this way from the beginning." (Matthew 19:7–8)

So in the case of remarriage, I knew that God's *perfect* will had been defeated, but His *permissive* will allowed me to achieve His purpose for my life.

Oswald Chambers, in his book *My Utmost for His Highest*, teaches us this distinction: "Always make a distinction between God's perfect will and His permissive will, which He uses to accomplish His divine purpose for our lives. God's perfect will is unchangeable. It is with His permissive will, or the various things that He allows into our lives, that we must wrestle before Him. It is our reaction to these things allowed by His permissive will that enables us to come to the point of seeing His perfect will for us."[11]

Keep a Daily Record

Sometimes in this portion of our ASK prayer journey, the way God is illuminating the path or answering our prayer is obvious and we are able to move quickly toward a solution. Other times, movement trickles in day by day, almost going unnoticed. This is where I've found it particularly helpful to keep a daily record of any movement in my prayer. One definition of *observe* is "to watch, view, or note for a scientific, official, or other special purpose."[12] If my ASK were part of a scientific research project, observing daily changes and taking note of those changes would be mandatory to determine the success of the project. So why don't we do the same with our prayers?

In a recent ASK of mine, I started a Notes page on my phone because things seemed to be occurring frequently and I didn't want to miss one. Later I transferred the list to my journal and added a few more things from emails and other correspondence. My recent ASK pertained to a ministry I had begun, and I was seeking God about whether I should proceed with it on a small scale or apply for 501(c)(3) status and incorporate it as a nonprofit organization. After beginning my thirty days of prayer, I noted the following movement:

> Day 1: Posted my note cards.
>
> Day 4: Two needs were presented by single moms I'm serving related to housing and employment, where my ministry doesn't have resources.
>
> Day 5: An agency who can facilitate the 501(c)(3) process called and emailed me with a discounted opportunity.
>
> Day 7: A leader from another church reached out to see if she could attend and learn from us.
>
> Day 7: Another ministry leader offered discount tickets for a goals workshop to our attendees.

Day 8: A new volunteer texted me with creative ideas and support for the next meeting.

Day 10: Another volunteer created excellent content and videoed at her own cost for our meeting.

Day 11: One of our core team members brought cross magnets (designed with ASK 7:7) made by a friend who was moved by the ministry to use as giveaways for the attendees.

Day 14: One of our ministry attendees gave a testimony about how it was changing her life and donated to the organization.

Day 14: A friend from a previous church heard about a ministry need and volunteered to help.

Day 16: Another leader (from a second church) asked to attend next month and learn from us.

And that was just the first sixteen days of this thirty-day prayer exercise! As I was reading over my journal listing of all God was showing me as I observed, my husband said, "It's like everything is happening with this ministry all at once." I reminded him that it was my focus of prayer for thirty days. Coincidence? I don't think so. I believe God was moving hearts and people to remind me that this ministry was important to Him and that I should press forward.

What if I had not been keeping a record? The month might have flown by with a lot of activity but without me seeing any of that movement related to my ASK. This is what I believe Paul was reminding the Colossians about it when he wrote, "Devote yourselves to prayer, being watchful and thankful" (4:2). If we pray being watchful, we will observe movement and take notes. If we pray being thankful, we will be reminded God is moving in response to our ASKs.

Each step of *search, explore, examine,* and *keep record* helps us to give focused attention while seeking God's answer to our prayer. Our lives are lived at such a fast pace; we are continually multitasking and flipping from one calendar page to another. Slowing down to observe what God is doing in our midst always makes the way clearer and illuminates our next steps.

ASK in Your Life

1. How can you use the question "Will it bless others or just me?" and Psalm 139:23–24 to help you in the *search* phase of seeking?

2. Pray and ask, "What else am I missing, God?" As you *explore* potential solutions to an ASK with Him, commit to being open to His leading.

3. What Scriptures can help you answer the questions "God, is this pathway one that pleases You?" and "Does this line up with Your will?" in the *examine* phase of seeking?

4. When *keeping record*, what tools would work best for you to observe, journal, and track what God might be saying about a current or future ASK?

CHAPTER 9

SEEK AND DO
THE NEXT RIGHT THING

When I think about the prayer seasons in my life and how the strategy of ASK has been filled with a lot of steps between *ask* and *receive*, it reminds me that this waiting period is not as passive as one would think.

Sometimes the answer to our prayer or clarity doesn't come for years, yet we must continue doing the next right thing. Jesus modeled this during His short thirty-three years on earth. One time, after healing Jairus's daughter from the sleep of death in Mark 5, Jesus told her to get up, and then while her parents and His disciples were standing astonished, He told them to bring her something to eat. Something to eat! Not, "Let's mark this momentous occasion with a praise or song or sermon about the wages of sin being death." Just, "Bring the girl something to eat" (see v. 43). I love how practical and earthly this instruction was after a miraculous healing. A simple, nourishing meal was the next right thing for Jairus's daughter.

One time that I just did the next right thing was during the engineering company merger that I briefly mentioned in chapter 7. My fourteen-year career with the corporation would come to an end on

December 31 due to this business decision. The merger team offered me a new position in Atlanta, Georgia, but our family committed to stay in Charlotte. My VP proposed that if I effectively closed the Charlotte office (which would take about four months of packing and handling sensitive personnel issues), they would pay me a year's severance as a bonus. Never in my forty-five years had I been blessed with such a generous amount of paid time off! I believed that this would be a great opportunity to take the seminary and corporate chaplaincy courses I had always dreamed of but had been unable to pursue because of work and family demands.

My husband and I prayed about it, researched the costs, and believed God confirmed the ASK with several close friends. One leader from our church confirmed seminary study as my next step as he quoted this verse, leading me to study God's Word further: "Your word is a lamp for my feet, a light on my path" (Psalm 119:105). This church leader also contributed toward my tuition. I completed three online seminary courses through Trinity Theological Seminary and during the same year got certified as a corporate chaplain through Corporate Chaplains of America (CCA). There were many part-time and full-time corporate chaplaincy openings in the Charlotte area, so this seemed to be a great career path for me to transition into.

However, near the end of my classwork and severance package, Gibson received a job offer from the Navy in Charleston. After we moved to Charleston and I settled the family in our new house, I called CCA to get started with corporate chaplaincy. I was shocked and frustrated that there were no chaplaincy positions anywhere in the low country. I pursued another national chaplaincy company but was rejected because I had been previously divorced. What was *that* about, God? I knew He'd led me to get certified, and I felt that was to be my next career.

Meanwhile we were still trying to sell our home in Charlotte and carrying two mortgages. One daughter was getting married that year and a second one was starting college. We needed the income. So I brushed up my résumé and did the next right thing. In a new city without previously established networks, apps, or online searches, it took several months of putting my résumé out there. But then I got a job. Not a corporate job like the one I had in Charlotte, and not a job in ministry using the courses I'd just completed, but an office manager job for a small family-owned business. A job providing steady income to help meet our obligations was the answer for my next step, using my office management skills from my past. I didn't think it would be a forever job or even a five-year job, but it introduced us to a beautiful family who helped make our transition to the low country less difficult. It's almost as if Anna from *Frozen 2* was guiding me with her lyrics from the song "The Next Right Thing," even though it was produced seventeen years later. When the char-acter Anna sings about taking a step again, she elaborates that sometimes that step is the next right thing.

Can you remember a time when doing the next right thing felt like a step backward, but then later you realized it was just a pause? Perhaps it was in your career or in a decision about your education. You could be facing one of those decisions in your current prayer journey, and wisdom tells you there's a next right thing. Don't be discouraged in taking the step if you believe it's the right one.

> **Can you remember a time when doing the next right thing felt like a step backward, but then later you realized it was just a pause?**

Remember that "he who began a good work in you will carry it on to completion" (Philippians 1:6). You'll hear more about how God did this for me with my chaplaincy certification in a later chapter!

Seek Until the Branches of the River Dry Up

There's a difference between taking the next right step when it lines up with God's best for our lives and becoming stuck because the right path is no longer in front of us. In my late twenties, when I was in a mini revival of my faith, there was a man in my office (I'll call him Kirk) who knew I was searching. I didn't share anything personal, but that's how it is with people who are walking in the Spirit. They often just know. I didn't know where he went to church or anything about his specific beliefs, but I knew he followed Jesus. There was a lightness in his countenance and a bounce in his steps that accompanied his pleasant nature, but he could also turn serious when needed. He would walk over to my desk under the pretense of getting candy from my crystal dish but then would linger long enough for me to dangle a question. So one day as he finished one butterscotch and went for the second, I dropped a big question: "How do you know if you're in the will of God?"

He paused for a minute and then said, "Have you ever been on a canoe in a river?"

I nodded, even though most of my canoe experiences were on a lake.

Kirk continued, "You might be in the main channel or the body of the river when suddenly you come to a branch or a fork. If you follow one branch, it might divert you for some time, but then it leads you back into the river. Sometimes, though, if you follow the wrong branch, it becomes a tributary or a smaller creek that eventually dries up. You have to go back the way you came to be in the main channel of the river and follow the flow."

Well, thanks, Kirk, for that geography lesson, but how does that relate to God's will?

He explained, "When you're in the will of God, there is movement and flow, and you know you've taken the right path because you are moving forward. But if you reach a dead end—like the drying up of a tributary—there is no water to continue canoeing, and you will have to go back and choose another tributary."

This reminded me of the story of Jonah in the Old Testament and how taking the wrong path went for him. God told Jonah to preach to a foreign city (Jonah 1:1–2), but he disobeyed. That disobedience got him thrown overboard by a frightened crew of sailors (vv. 14–15), swallowed alive by a mammoth fish in the ocean (v. 17), and then miraculously spit out three days later (2:10). That sounds like several dead ends in the river, doesn't it? Jonah then preached to the people in the foreign city, they listened to him, and God showed them mercy because of it. Jonah's initial disobedience took him not to dry land at the end of a channel but into the belly of a huge fish!

Sometimes disobedience on our part can come from just not paying attention or asking God. On the day of my first wedding, I remember being in the bride's room getting ready with my bridesmaids, and no one seemed happy. They weren't sad, but neither were they happy. Then I realized it was because I wasn't happy. Not happy in the way I always imagined I would be on my wedding day. My mood affected everyone in the room. I had been away from God in the years leading up to this day, so it had not dawned on me to ask Him about a spouse or whether I should even get married. So in those hours just before that solemn vow, I realized too late that my lack of happiness correlated to the lack of seeking God for direction in my life. I wasn't receiving the Holy Spirit's guidance during those years, so I wasn't observant about the dry path I was on. Somewhere between the girl of sixteen who'd pledged her life to God and this day at age twenty-two were too many years of a young woman who was angry and distant with Him. With few godly influences or Christian mentors, there was no one to ask me critical questions about being unequally yoked (see 2 Corinthians 6:14). I walked down the aisle—or swam down a channel—that ended ten years later in a dried-up tributary. But like Jonah, God redeemed my willful wrong choice with two daughters who bring life and hope to thousands of others.

Whether you choose outright disobedience or take the wrong path by accident, it's critical to realize when the channel has become dry and then to ask God for correction. But please hear me about my choice resulting in divorce: There were many years of counseling and many personal stories involved in how God allowed my divorce. I won't share that story here, but I just want to be clear that I know that God hates divorce and that He holds the marriage covenant high.

Just because you're in a dry season of marriage doesn't mean it was the wrong choice or a poor one that God cannot redeem. Get wise Christian counsel and pursue the marriage covenant, as much as it is up to you. Of course, if a marriage has abuse or abandonment, the covenant is already broken.

Open Doors, Closed Doors

Sometimes the path we are praying about is so unclear that our prayer becomes less specific. In those situations, I've prayed this passage: ". . . the words of the holy one, the true one, who has the key of David, who opens and no one will shut, who shuts and no one opens" (Revelation 3:7 ESV).

One friend says that we should pray for open doors without trying to knock down any that are closed. That's good for a person who likes to take action (like me) to hear, because sometimes a closed door seems like just another challenge to tackle. Knocking down a closed door might look like continuing with a decision even when a trusted spiritual leader or pastor doesn't think it's wise. Or you may be knocking down a closed door if you're placing your personal interests above those of others. As a mother of adult children, putting aside our interests is one the most difficult things we do, but sometimes it's necessary.

This prayer helps me when praying for a loved one's situation when I know it's difficult to put my personal interests aside. Once when my daughter Jess and son-in-law Nick were praying about moving their family from the East Coast to Seattle, Washington, I found it difficult to pray for their move. If I was being honest with God, there was no way I wanted them to relocate to the other side of the United States from us. I had never lived that far away from family and couldn't imagine them doing that either.

I found myself praying, "God, open doors that only You can open and close doors that only You can close." I knew Jess and Nick were listening to God and looking for His confirmation. By praying those words, I knew that if this move was not from Him, the closed doors would stop it from happening. He didn't close any doors of employment, housing, or travel arrangements during the decision process. As a matter of fact, they felt great confirmation from a variety of sources, including Scripture and trusted elders. It was exceedingly hard for me to be that far away from them, but we all survived those years of physical separation. It's also easier to see in hindsight how God used their years in Seattle as seeds for future years in ministry.

Another loved one's relocation involved our daughter Caroline and the COVID-19 pandemic. Furloughed for twelve weeks, Caroline spent several months with us in South Carolina, since she knew being with the community of family would be better than quarantining alone in her apartment in Orlando. Once she was called back to work remotely, Caroline prayed about moving back to Charleston so she could be near family while working remotely for the company she loved. Her dad and I started the ASK process alongside Caroline, but of course I wanted her to be near us instead of an eight-hour drive away.

While we helped her with the tactical parts of *seek*, like finding an affordable apartment in Charleston and doing a budget, we knew that only God could see into her future. My prayers became "Open doors, close doors" with every breath. After she walked through all the proper channels with human resources for relocation, the answer became more cloudy.

Caroline called one day. "The doors are not opening up. My company doesn't know when we will be called back to our offices, but when they do call us back, I will be responsible for breaking a lease. That is definitely a closed door for me."

I knew that God had closed doors for her move to South Carolina, but He had opened doors in her prayer life. Almost one year after she made that decision, her company formalized their remote-working policies and she needed to be located within one hour of the corporate office. God knew what was the best decision for her long-term living situation and gave her peace before the company gave her clarity.

Whether you are clear about which channel is the one flowing or wondering whether to try another path, the most critical thing is to know the Source of the channel and to seek Him about doing the next right thing. Keeping God as our source makes the decision tree simple for us as believers. I ran across this poem I wrote in those years of learning about the next right step and geography lessons from Kirk, so at least I was on the right track:

The Force of the Flow

Babbling brook, clear and strong
Take me back where I belong.
Running free past stumbling stones,
Gurgling aloud with a glorious song.
Where is the energy? Where is the source?
This zest for life that I love most.
It begins at the top—from a hole in the ground—
This joy of creation, which man has now found.

Though sometimes it stops
When blocked on its way,
The Force carries it onward
Day after day.

ASK in Your Life

1. When was a time that doing the next right thing felt like a step backward, but then later you realized it was just a pause? How does Philippians 1:6 bring comfort about the pause?

2. Read Jonah 1 and note how many times Jonah was redirected because he wasn't in the will of God.

3. When was a time that you were angry with God? Maybe you're angry with Him now and stuck in a dry channel of the river. Confess your anger and repent. In the coming days, see if God opens a new path.

4. How might praying "open doors, close doors" help you in the seek portion of an ASK? This is another area where journaling daily will be helpful in discerning if the doors are opening or closing in a situation.

CHAPTER 10

SEEK FOR CONFIRMATION

I f we are paying attention to God's Word and His voice, God is always speaking and telling us how to take the next steps. But the world's voice sometimes gets louder, and even our own critical thinking can get in the way of doing what we know. If there's any confusion on our part—even though God has spoken—praying for confirmation can be helpful.

Fleece or Fleeces?

One way to seek God's confirmation is by praying a fleece. If you're a new believer, you may have heard this phrase before and wondered, "What is a fleece, and why would I pray one?" If you're not familiar with Gideon and his fleeces before God, go to Judges 6 with a hot cuppa and settle in for a great read. I won't repeat the entire story here, just the part about the fleece:

> Gideon said to God, "If you will save Israel by my hand as you have promised—look, I will place a wool fleece on the threshing floor. If there is dew only on the fleece and all the ground is dry, then I will know that you will save Israel by my hand, as you said." And that is what happened.

Gideon rose early the next day; he squeezed the fleece and wrung out the dew—a bowlful of water.

Then Gideon said to God, "Do not be angry with me. Let me make just one more request. Allow me one more test with the fleece, but this time make the fleece dry and let the ground be covered with dew." That night God did so. Only the fleece was dry; all the ground was covered with dew. (Judges 6:36–40)

It's worth noting two important facts in the story:

1. God had already spoken to Gideon three times and told him what to do (vv. 12, 14, 16). It was Gideon's need to confirm this command from God that led him to put out a fleece.
2. Gideon reversed the fleece request just to make sure he wasn't misinterpreting an event related to nature.

Some theologians call Gideon's fleece a test of God or a lack of faith. I try to remember this when asking God for confirmation through a fleece or a sign. There have been a few occasions in my life, though, when the decision ahead of me was so impactful to our family, I prayed like Gideon and our merciful God answered.

A Fleece to Direct and Protect

As I review my prayer-life history, there have been only two times in my sixtyish years when I put out a fleece before God to confirm a decision. Both times involved a job change. Maybe that's because job changes are where we are most vulnerable to the things of the world (income, position, placement), or maybe those were just times I most needed Him to speak loudly. The first time I put out a fleece was when my job was coming to an end due to the engineering company merger. As my last day on the job was nearing, I received an offer from one of the VPs for a job at a new company he was starting. This VP and I had partnered together to lead a global task force. I respected his business acumen and had seen up close his ability to lead with vision. He was starting a new risk insurance company and approached me to help him launch and run it. It was an attractive offer financially, and I knew it would provide well for our family. Plus, I could bank the year of severance from my old job and keep working. But I couldn't take this job offer and do the online seminary study I had planned to pursue. I was confused. So that night when I prayed about the decision before me, I put out a fleece: "God, if this is from you, have the VP call me before noon tomorrow."

This wasn't completely out of the ordinary; he had been calling me every few days to talk about the job possibility. But it was a fleece—or a stretch—because he usually called late in the afternoon. The next day, I sat in my office for most of the morning, waiting on his call and also wondering if God thought me silly for asking something so specific. I was clearly torn about this offer and confused about what God had originally told me to do next, which was to attend seminary online and pursue chaplaincy. Much like Gideon, I believed that God wanted me to step out in faith and do the hard thing.

So I waited. At 12:01 p.m., I sighed a huge sigh of relief and took a deep breath to begin my new journey of seminary study. Later that day, the VP called, and I turned down his job offer. Was God directing me with the timing of a phone call? I believe so with all my heart. This VP went on to form the new company, and it was wildly successful at the start. Until about three years later, when I read that the company had gone bankrupt and closed their doors. Without asking God about my next steps, I would've sought the temporary financial reward of a salary and staying employed instead of an unclear future studying His Word. For a former single mom, everything about a steady paycheck seemed to be the safer choice for me at the time. I needed God's confirmation on which direction. Many times we won't know or see the reality of God's protection until years later or even until heaven. In this case, though, God not only directed me but allowed me to see a few years later how He protected me from making a decision based on the security of income.

Fleeces for Big Moves

Another time I used a fleece was with Gibson's opportunity to take a job with the Navy in Charleston. We had planned to stay in the Charlotte area as most of our family lived there and our roots were deep. But since our severance checks were running out and we had three daughters, we opened our minds to the idea of relocating. Gibson and I traveled to Charleston the first week of December for his interview. There had been Scriptures God had given us in the weeks leading up to this, and we both felt that this job and relocation were what God had in mind for us.

But moving would be a big upheaval for this native Charlottean, especially during a season when we were leaving elderly parents behind. Like before, we felt God's leading but needed more confirmation. One of my prayers was that Gibson's next supervisor would be a Christian. I know we're not always going to be surrounded by Christians in the workplace, and that is part of being "salt and light" (Matthew 5:13–16), but his last couple of assignments had been demanding, and his supervisors were not life-giving or family focused.

On this December interview trip, my fleece was this: "God, let us know if this new supervisor is a Christian before Gibson goes any further in the interview process." At the end of a long day of team interviews, Gibson reported that his interviewing supervisor had prayed over their meal at lunch and shared about a church that his family visited the previous day. Go, God! He answered my fleece with a clear confirmation. There were many other ways God confirmed this move within in the next months, but the fleece was so personal and specific, it left no doubt in my mind.

Seeking a Sign

Maybe you have a big decision to make and have done the due diligence of praying ahead of time and then making lists of pros and cons. Everything seems to be adding up to take the next step, but you'd really like God to confirm the decision with a sign. Some might say this is asking too much from the God of the universe to give us a sign, but for those who are parents, I know you'll agree that you would always welcome a child coming to you for wisdom no matter how large or small the decision.

A sign is slightly different from a fleece in that it lacks the same level of specificity. When I've prayed a fleece before God, I have asked for particular outcomes that would let me know God was in the decision, like a phone call before a specific time. If the decision I'm praying about is less weighty (not affecting others' futures) but still important to get God's confirmation, I will often ask Him for a sign.

An employment opportunity for me that left me wanting a sign was after we had lived in Charleston for a few years. After serving as an office manager for a small company, I desired a more challenging position closer to my level of experience. I responded to an ad for a CFO for a large nonprofit that seemed to be in my wheelhouse. It would also stretch my skills and require a significant amount of time each week and a longer commute. After the interview, it felt like God was leading me to this position for growth. There was also a significant pay increase, which was much needed in this season of college and wedding expenses.

So as I walked the beach that weekend with Gibson, I asked God to give me a sign to take the new job. I had always looked for and wanted to find sand dollars at this Isle of Palms beach but had never seen any. Suddenly, we stumbled across a stretch of beach with hundreds of sand dollars lying face up on the sand. I gingerly picked one up and lifted my head to praise God, because the organization I just interviewed with had the symbol of a sand dollar on its website and on all printed company material. Silly coincidence or God answering with a sign through nature? I believe that in this case, God's creation became God's confirmation.

Clear Confirmation

As I've demonstrated by having just a few examples from my lifetime, seeking with a fleece or for a sign shouldn't be our default method of seeking God's confirmation on an ask. We have two things in this present age that weren't available to Gideon: the Bible and spiritual mentors led by the Holy Spirit. Confirmation of an answered prayer doesn't happen in a vacuum, and that's the beautiful thing about seeing how God speaks and answers us through many forms. These are two primary ways we can look to God to confirm an answer to prayer when trying to discern our next steps:

1. The answer lines up with God's Word. If the answer you think you're hearing is from God, it will always align with truth from the Bible. You're never going to hear an answer from God that is in direct contrast to His commandments or instructions. This first step keeps us from running off the rails with decisions or perceived answers that wouldn't please God but might instead be self-serving. Paul tells us this in Philippians 4:9: "Whatever you have learned or received or heard from me, or seen in me—put it into practice. And the God of peace will be with you." Another word on this is found in 2 Timothy 3:16: "All Scripture is God-breathed and is useful for teaching, rebuking, correcting and training in righteousness." The more familiar we are with God's Word, the better we will know His voice.

> **Confirmation of an answered prayer doesn't happen in a vacuum, and that's the beautiful thing about seeing how God speaks and answers us through many forms.**

2. The answer is confirmed by trusted elders or spiritual mentors when you ask for their wisdom on the question. This is taught in Ephesians 3:10: ". . . so that through the church the manifold wisdom of God might now be made known to the rulers and authorities in the heavenly places" (ESV). Titus 2 is a great chapter on mentorship and finding spiritual mentors for both

men and women. Also in 2 Timothy 2:2 we read, "What you have heard from me in the presence of many witnesses entrust to faithful men, who will be able to teach others also" (ESV). Knowing that spiritual mentors, pastors, and counselors have walked with God for a period of time, and that they study the Bible regularly, gives us confidence to know they won't recommend something that disagrees with God's Word.

This last portion of seeking—seeking for confirmation—is most critical because while seeking requires us to take action, it's important to refrain from being too independent in the process. This last step reminds me to follow the old saying, "Pray as though everything depended on God. Work as though everything depended on you."

And in the practice of ask, seek, and knock, I would add to the saying: "And seek confirmation from God after you've done the work."

ASK in Your Life

1. Read Judges 6 about Gideon and his fleece. If you're familiar with the story, try reading in a translation different from your usual. What might a modern-day fleece look like for you?

2. How familiar are you with the Scriptures? If you know the Bible well, where might you look to hear God's answer to your ASK? If you don't know it well, how can you take one small step to become more familiar with it?

3. Do you have spiritual mentors you can go to for wisdom and confirmation of an answer to prayer? If not, read Titus 2 and brainstorm a list of people who might serve in that role for you. If you do have spiritual mentors, what ask do you need to confide to them and seek advice about?

4. Praying for confirmation can help us from leaping into action too soon with what we believe is God's answer to our ASK. What prayer are you currently praying that needs you to pause for confirmation in one of the ways mentioned in this chapter?

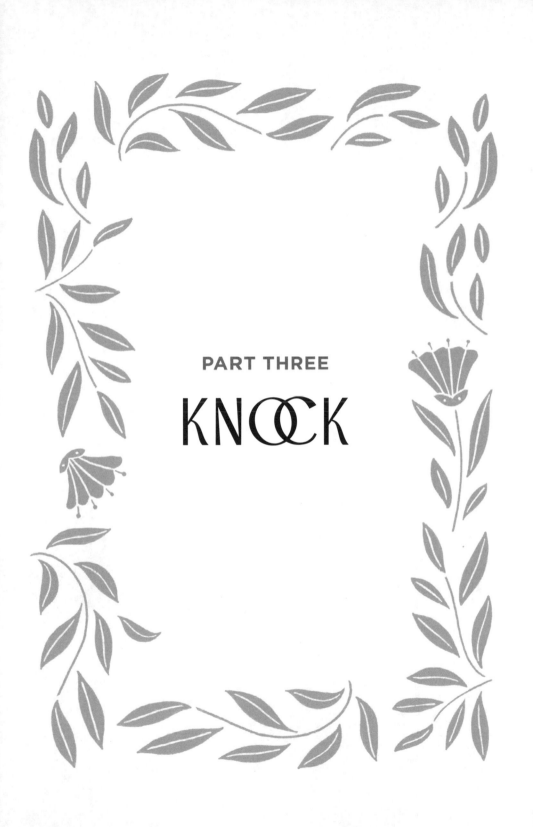

PART THREE

KNOCK

CHAPTER 11

KNOCKING FORMS MUSCLES

The last part of the ASK model for prayer in Matthew 7:7 is the most physical, can take the most time, and requires the most persistence. The Greek word in this verse for "knock" is an active verb that can mean "to keep on knocking." So it goes with many of my prayers during the *knock* portion of my ASK journeys. The time it takes during the knock portion is sometimes discouraging for those of us who are action oriented and can cause one to stop praying. Unlike the *seek* portion of praying, where we are actively observing and searching for an answer, the largest part of knocking is waiting. Knocking also implies that someone must open the door. Maybe it's my Southern upbringing, but there's hardly ever a time when I will knock on a door and then open it without waiting. With these parameters in mind about what it means to knock on a door, let's look at what's involved in knocking with a request before God.

Spinning Your Wheels

I have a love-hate relationship with my spin bike. We purchased it a few years ago when I realized my outdoor bike was too dependent on weather and traffic. What I love most about it is that it's available 24-7 and does not require a gym membership or instructor since the online classes are there for my strength and duration selection. Within a few minutes of putting on the right shoes, going up to our guest room, and logging in, I can be cycling in Norway or Spain and then be back to my other tasks within minutes of finishing a session. I also love that cycling strengthens my quads without burdening my weak knee, so this low-impact exercise is perfect for me.

> Some of the hardest and longest prayer ASKs that I've put before the Father were also the ones that built strength for the next time I tackled a new prayer request.

You might be thinking, That sounds perfect! What's not to love about that setup? The catch is that it requires consistency to be effective. I can choose to spin one day one week, but the next week when I get back on, it's like I'm starting over building strength and muscles. Then I find myself in a continuous loop of beginner cycling without ever building on the previous session.

The knock portion of my prayer journey is much the same. Some of the hardest and longest prayer ASKs that I've put before the Father were also the ones that built strength for the next time I tackled a new prayer request. These answers to prayer took years and years, but when God answered in a way that only He could, it encouraged me to continue knocking.

One time that knocking formed muscles in my prayer life was during my years of praying for my oldest daughter. Katie was raised in the church and served as a leader in her youth group. She performed in youth musicals, went through confirmation, danced in the liturgical choir, and attended summer camps, so she was no stranger to church. Katie was also popular, pretty, and fun loving, so in high school this translated into a lot of opportunities outside of church settings. Though I had tried to provide a stable home environment as a single mom, I was also working full-time and traveling for business during her preteen years. As mothers, we tend to take responsibility for all the choices our children make, when in fact the world is fallen and full of trouble around every corner.

That said, the choices that led to Kate being a rebellious teen are her story. The prayer muscles formed during those years are mine.

I tried all the regular tricks, including parenting classes, counseling, strict curfews, grounding, taking away privileges, and an unhealthy amount of screaming and slamming doors (yes, on my part sadly). I was also praying during this time, but even my prayers were designed to try to control Katie, not to ask God to change her from the inside out. Some prayers were targeted at behaviors while others named friends or boys I was trying to pray out of her life.

These days were hard for both of us. I've never had a poker face, so Katie could see my disapproval every time she came in after curfew or was caught in a situation that wasn't her best. I wish I could tell you that I silently cried out to God from a prayer closet, but there were a few years of trying to chase Katie down and then crying out to God afterward.

Where Two or More Form Muscles

A huge refocusing of my prayers began when a group of moms started meeting during church youth group to pray for our teens. I've always believed in the power of praying together with other believers, and this time we lived it out on Wednesday nights.

Not only is there power in gathering people to pray, but it helps focus your prayers—it certainly did for me. It was a lot harder to try to pray people out of Katie's life when I had to speak those requests aloud to other moms. Slowly my prayers became focused on having Jesus come into her life in a real and personal way. These moms heard my ragged cries to God in a way that was humbling, but the praying also started a release. I began releasing control of Katie's outward behavior and asked God to rescue her in a way that only He could.

Since one of my prayers had been to get the troublemakers out of her life, I started praying the opposite. Instead of praying certain people out, I began praying that she would see some godly young adults as cool and likable. By that time in my parenting, I knew that while I didn't have much influence over her, many others would, and I prayed they would be the right someones. One godly influence became evident early during those years, and I was convinced this was an immediate answer to my prayers. The organization Young Life had a strong presence at Katie's high school, and one of their leaders, Ashley Mink Kimbrough, was pursuing her. Ashley would stop by during Katie's lunchtime in the cafeteria or show up when she was in the homecoming parade or for other special occasions. Katie seemed to listen to Ashley and allow her access, but Katie's outward behavior and rebellious nature did not change. I still encouraged her participation in Young Life and her relationship with this mentor, but I no longer thought of it as a specific answer to my prayers.

Slipping Away or Drawing Close?

As Katie graduated from high school and enrolled in a major state university a hundred miles away, I saw any perceived control slipping through my fingers. But I continued to pray for roommates, suitemates, and activities that would tether her to a Christian walk. Even on dorm move-in weekend, I suggested the United Methodist Student Center might be a great place for her to visit on Sundays. Ha! Katie was free from my grasp and ready for all the freedom that college life had to offer.

But God. He never released His hold on her.

Within the first two months of university life, Katie was drawn to the idea of being a Young Life counselor at a high school near campus. Before she could be a Young Life counselor, Katie realized there were lifestyle changes she had to make. It was during this time that she had what I believe was a true conversion experience. Again, the details of Katie's rebirth in the Spirit are her story, but the outcome is all to God's glory.

She called one night to tell me about her conversion and talked of Scriptures that were coming alive for her. Her voice seemed different, softer and more loving. On her next trip home, Katie's face shone with the light of Jesus.

Since that day, I have continued to marvel at how God has kept His hold on her. God led her to Josh Walters, her husband of twenty years. God leads her in mothering seven incredible children. Josh serves as a pastor at a megachurch, and Katie also teaches and preaches God's Word on a regular basis. She founded and is CEO of an international mission, Francis + Benedict, based in Togo. This nonprofit organization employs and provides for seamstresses in West Africa and over two hundred women in the United States. Everything she does is from being tethered as a child of God, with Jesus as her Savior.

A New Thing

Could I have envisioned so much for rebellious Katie in her teen years? Never. But something in me kept hanging on to all the Scriptures I'd prayed for her. I've joked many times that God had to get her away from me to save her so I couldn't take any credit for it! The truth is that God's timing is His. The path to the outcome is God's plan too, whether or not we are able to perceive it. Isaiah 43:19 reminds us,

> See, I am doing a new thing!
>   Now it springs up; do you not perceive it?
> I am making a way in the wilderness
>   and streams in the wasteland.

In this passage God was promising (through His prophet Isaiah) that the Israelites would have a different rescue in the form of salvation. Today, it's still a reminder for us that God is always working and, as our Creator, is always doing new things.

If I had only been able to perceive it when Young Life and Ashley were making an impact on Katie's future way in the wilderness. I didn't see any immediate change in Katie's behavior, but she told me later it was Ashley's example that made her want to be a Young Life counselor. That mentorship ultimately led to her rebirth in Christ.

The struggles may seem to go on forever, and the answers to our ASK prayers sometimes take years and years. Those struggles may bruise us or leave scars, but they also form muscles. The muscles formed in my prayer life knocking for Katie's soul are some of my strongest prayer muscles today.

There are still unanswered prayers in my life that sometimes cause me to doubt if I should continue praying about that same ask. But Katie and God. He has given me the testimony of answered prayer over her life in a way that I could never ask or imagine, and I use it regularly to encourage myself and others. Many times when I speak to women, it's the testimony of Katie that speaks to the mothers in the room. Maybe you're one of those moms right now and have a rebellious teenager or an adult child who seems far from God. Have you been knocking without seeing answers to your prayers? Surrender them to God. Ask Him to come into your child's life instead of trying to keep others out. Knock on God's door day and night with tenacity. Don't accept what culture or well-meaning friends tell you about giving up. Never give up and never stop praying. You are building muscles!

Muscle Memory

The muscles you form in long-standing prayers will also form muscle memory. When a movement is repeated over time, the brain creates long-term muscle memory for that task, eventually allowing it to be performed with little to no conscious effort. So in the seventeen-plus years I was praying for Katie, those efforts formed muscle memory that allows me to pray more effectively today. During those difficult days of parenting and praying, I never thought of my prayer times as a workout—though I was on my knees a lot of nights. The muscle memory formed then allows me to pray more readily when someone randomly approaches me for prayer or when a stranger reaches out to me on social media. The muscle memory reminds me to stop what I'm doing or even pray as I'm going, because I know two things: (1) God answers prayers for our prodigals, and (2) the rewards are great if we can just perceive what He is doing.

Muscle memory is typically found in many everyday activities that become automatic and improve with practice, such as riding bicycles. That means it's time for me to get back on my spin bike to form some new physical muscles. Sometimes the hardest habits to restart require us to take that first step or first spin. Have you been discouraged by seemingly unanswered prayers? Pick up your ASK note cards and continue knocking on God's door. He promises to open it. I've got the muscles and the muscle memory to prove it.

ASK in Your Life

1. What ASK in your prayer life could be building your muscles? How does identifying this long-standing prayer as strength training help you in the waiting?

2. Sometimes in the midst of life's challenges we can't perceive the path leading to God's best outcome. Meditate on Isaiah 43:19 while asking Him what "new thing" He is doing in your life. Even if it's not obvious right now, go ahead and praise God for this new thing.

3. Think of a friend who has been asking in prayer for a long time, perhaps for a rebellious child or a prodigal. Encourage them with a note, text, or reminder not to give up as they build muscles of prayer.

4. As we use treadmills and weights to build physical muscles, we can use ASK note cards as a similar tool to build prayer muscle memory. What prayer seems stagnant right now and needs an application of the note cards?

CHAPTER 12

KNOCKING IS LOUD

In this day of doorbells, Ring cameras, and texting when we arrive somewhere, we may not even knock on a door to enter a house. But that wasn't the case in Jesus's day. You knocked squarely on the door so the person inside would hear you. When Jesus said, "Knock and the door will be opened" (Matthew 7:7), He was referring to a loud, audible knock.

I've given this a lot of thought as I've written "ask," "seek," and "knock" on my index cards over the years. As Jesus was teaching His followers how to pray, He knew believers today wouldn't have physical access to Him. Instead, the knocking is symbolic of a step in our prayer process. As knocking had to be loud to get the attention of the person inside, so this is also when our prayers get loud. There are several ways my ASKs have been loud and helped expand my reach beyond posting an index card on my bathroom mirror.

Getting Loud with Others

When a family member is near death, it's natural to ask others to pray. I wrote about my sister Barbara's brush with death and ARDS in chapter 5 and how we had churches praying for her healing. Thankfully, email was up and running strong in 1996, and we emailed prayer chains at seventy-five churches and workplaces across the southeast. The praying started with our local churches in Charlotte, but soon relatives and friends of Barbara's were also asking their churches to pray. My emails to each of these churches included weekly updates on Barbara's condition along with some specific asks for next steps in her recovery.

I posted the emails in her ICU room along with cards we received so that the doctors and nurses would know many prayers were being lifted up for Barbara and for their healing touch on her. Many of the nurses were moved by the prayers and read what we were taping to the windows of her unit. Others read them aloud to Barbara; as they stated, it is important to talk to someone in a coma.

Prayers for Barbara's healing were no longer silent or singular. If those forty-plus churches had an average of just ten people praying, there were four hundred people praying for a woman they had never met. Today, it's much simpler to share a prayer need using social media. We've all seen how a family in crisis will suddenly reach thousands or hundreds of thousands by posting a photo and updates on Facebook or Instagram. That's some powerful knocking! When we pray for someone and those prayers are loud, we create the possibility for others to get involved in the prayer. Posting the churches' prayers on Barbara's ICU walls was a time when praying loudly resulted in gaining the attention of others, and some of those people joined us in prayer. I know God is jazzed to have more people praying.

When we pray for someone and those prayers are loud, we create the possibility for others to get involved in the prayer.

Loud and Fervent Prayers

Another time my knocking in prayer got loud was during my single-again years after my first marriage ended. After a season of being the only adult in the house, I yearned for companionship and remarriage. My journals from those years show the struggles of dating and wondering if God had someone just for me. One journal entry shows my impatience clearly:

> I'm lonely, Lord. I need a playmate—someone to have fun with—and potentially a strong male for Katie and Jessie to learn from and also see a husband and wife partnership. I'm trusting and trying very hard to be patient. I believe that you are getting someone ready for me—but is that in my immediate future or distant? If it's distant, I need you to take away the ache again.

Then a few more pages over, I echo the same refrain. Loneliness. Heartache. Questioning. Though I didn't involve four hundred people praying for this need, I was loud with God in my journaled prayers. I was crying out fervently—and often—in case He did not hear me the last time I asked (at least that's what it felt like!).

Obviously God's character doesn't change with the intensity or repetition of our prayers. But maybe there's some part of our character that changes when we pray fervently and often for the same thing. With my prayers for a spouse, the nature of my prayers subtly shifted from anger to doubt to acceptance. It was only when my prayers shifted to an acceptance of either outcome (singleness or remarriage) that I saw God's answers to this fervent prayer.

Is there something you've been praying for with intensity and for a long duration? Have you noticed any shifts in your character as you've approached God? Maybe in the way you've worded your prayer differently or in the questions you ask Him?

David Knocked Loudly

When I go back and read my journal entries, they sometimes seem whiny or repetitive. Then I remember many of the psalms written by David. Of the 150 psalms in the Bible, 75 are attributed to David, and many of those are ones of worship or praise. But there are an equal number where David is crying out loudly to God. Many of those psalms are known as psalms of lament. Psalm 22 is a great example of how David lamented and, much like single-again Deb, didn't believe God was listening or heard him.

As we look at Psalm 22 in the English Standard Version, it's also easy to see the up-and-down transitions in David's emotions as he prayed loudly to God. The first verses clearly show his anguish in not feeling heard:

> My God, my God, why have you forsaken me?
>> Why are you so far from saving me, from the words of
>>> my groaning?
> O my God, I cry by day, but you do not answer,
>> and by night, I find no rest. (vv. 1–2)

Then David shifts to praising God in verse 3, "Yet you are holy, enthroned on the praises of Israel," before he moves to degradation in verses 6 and 7:

> But I am a worm and not a man,
>> scorned by mankind and despised by the people.
> All who see me mock me;
>> they make mouths at me; they wag their heads.

The next section is where David seems to remember and speak life about who he is, created by God. But then he slips back into reminding God about his problems in verses 12 to 18. A last fervent plea comes verses 19 to 21:

> But you, O Lord, do not be far off!
>> O you my help, come quickly to my aid!
> Deliver my soul from the sword,
>> my precious life from the power of the dog!
> Save me from the mouth of the lion!

Finally David's prayer stops all the back and forth and progresses into a steady stream of declarations, praise, and worship in the final stanzas of this psalm prayer.

At least single-again Deb did not get as descriptive as those verses! While I might've felt as if I lay "in the dust of death" (v. 15), those were not the words I wrote. Desperation causes us to cry out or press in with desperate measures, but hopefully we transition to hope as David did. A key element of biblical laments is that they move from lament to hope. We can remember that when knocking loudly, even in the midst of lament, we are crying out to the God of hope.

Bleeding for Twelve Years

When I think about my cries or the more descriptive ones of David, I am reminded of a woman in the Bible who used her physical presence to knock loudly. In Luke 8, we read about a woman who had been hemorrhaging for twelve years:

> A woman was there who had been subject to bleeding for twelve years, but no one could heal her. She came up behind him and touched the edge of his cloak, and immediately her bleeding stopped.
>
> "Who touched me?" Jesus asked.
>
> When they all denied it, Peter said, "Master, the people are crowding and pressing against you."
>
> But Jesus said, "Someone touched me; I know that power has gone out from me."
>
> Then the woman, seeing that she could not go unnoticed, came trembling and fell at his feet. In the presence of all the people, she told why she had touched him and how she had been instantly healed. Then he said to her, "Daughter, your faith has healed you. Go in peace." (vv. 43–48)

During biblical times, it was believed that a woman's menstrual bleeding made her ritually unclean. This story is unique in that "unclean" people were not allowed in public places. It took a lot of courage for this woman to show up in a public place, and even more for her to press in and touch Jesus's garment. But she was desperate, right? Desperate times call for desperate measures. Women are used to bleeding every month. But frequent, uncontrolled bleeding is a whole other level of suffering and pain that requires a loud knock. She took the risk of going against culturally accepted practices and "knocked" on Jesus's garment to get His attention. The result was not only her healing but Jesus's commendation to her when He said, "Daughter, your faith has healed you. Go in peace."

Risk versus Reward

There's a risk in going public and knocking loudly with our prayers, isn't there? We risk feeling foolish for asking or even worse if the prayers don't get answered the way we expect. When the prayers are for someone else—like my sister who was in a coma and near death—I don't consider the risk as much. It was still a little humbling to reach out to people for prayer when some of them were not church attenders. One of the emails I sent during those months praying for Barbara went to one of my coworkers at the global engineering firm. She was not a believing Christian but was willing to forward the email updates to those at the firm who were asking about Barbara. After Barbara was healed and going home from rehab, I got an email from this woman in response to my thank-you to her. She said:

> My instantaneous reply was "I didn't do anything." Later I thought of my remark, and then I thought, well I really did do something—one of the most important things of all—I PRAYED TO GOD. No, I didn't do more than anyone else who prayed for Barb, but I participated. I have faltered in believing in the power of prayer in the past. I have been guilty of saying, "God why aren't you listening to me?" But I have come a long way from that day. He's listening. I know that for sure now. I also joined the church and when I told my friend she said "My Sunday School class has been praying for you." So see, your prayers and

her prayers helped me. It really touched my heart when
you told me you were praying for me.

The rewards were great in knocking loudly with this friend, don't
you think?

Getting Personal

When an ASK gets personal, the risk giant rears its ugly head with
taunts. I recently had to get loud about a prayer request for myself
and must admit to some second thoughts about whether to get loud
or keep it to myself. I had come down with the omicron variant of
COVID-19 and was sick for only seven days. Soon after, though, I
noticed a continuous whooshing sound in my right ear that would
not go away. When I went to the ENT, the audiologist told me I
had 60 percent loss of hearing in my right ear, and the tinnitus was
the nerve's way of compensating for the loss. The doctors tried several regimens of steroids (both oral and shots into the eardrum) and
recommended that I reduce caffeine and sodium in case it was Mé-
nière's disease. Still the hearing was not returning, and the whooshing continued to be loud in my ear. My family and close friends had
been praying, but when the first round of shots didn't work, I felt it
was time to get loud with my ASK. I posted a video on Instagram
asking my social media friends to join me in praying for healing.
Within days almost three thousand people had viewed the video,
and there were over one hundred comments from people joining in
my ASK.

Want to know some of the rewards I experienced for knocking
loudly with my prayer? I heard from several people fighting the same
condition and, at the urging of a mutual friend, called one woman
to pray with her over the phone. One woman I barely knew wrote
to tell me that she and her husband spent time praying for me and
believed I would be healed. A couple of other people messaged to say
they had been suffering this same ailment in silence for years. There

were God moments just in posting about my ASK and encouragement and prayer for many beyond myself.

Eight weeks later, after receiving another round of shots and many prayers, I was able to post another video proclaiming God's healing of my ear. That video has now had almost five thousand views and fifty-plus comments giving praise to God. It was humbling and a little scary to ask by knocking loudly, but I believe God received glory both before and after the healing. If I had stayed silent with my ASK, no one would've had the privilege of praying with me, and very few would now be praising God and considering the ASK prayer model the next time they have a personal need.

Oh . . . I Get It!

One of our former pastors, Dr. David Chadwick, said that the most commonly heard phrase once we get to heaven will be "Oh . . . I get it!" Dr. Chadwick was referring to the many revelations we'll have in heaven about circumstances that were confusing or didn't make sense here on earth. This gives me great comfort when I don't see obvious answers to my prayers or lack understanding about the choices men and women make.

There certainly have been times when I didn't knock loudly enough with my ASKs. Sometimes I've prayed half-heartedly, without intensity. Other times I've focused on praying for a specific change but gave up when there were no immediate results. Or I've prayed without asking others to join me on the journey, selfishly tucking away God's answer without the added benefit of bringing more glory to Him. Maybe the same has been true for you? Let's not stoop to self-condemnation or regret about any prayers that have been uttered to the One who knows and hears all. Instead, let's bring intensity and fervor and hope to any prayer we've been voicing quietly for months or years. Let our hope be louder than our lamenting!

ASK in Your Life

1. Is there a prayer in your life where you need to get loud and include others? If not, envision some ways in the future to share an ASK through social media or email when it's an urgent need and requires many intercessors.

2. Maybe your ask is more personal and necessitates you getting loud with God in your conversational prayers or journaling to Him. Read Psalm 22, then journal your ask in the margins of each section of that psalm.

3. Do you find yourself transitioning to hope after your loud knocking? If not, read more of David's psalms and try to emulate his laments. Writing out your prayers will help you focus on how much of them is lament and when you shift to hope.

4. Maybe there's someone who will join with you in praying, and God will bless them as a result. Stop right now and ask God who that person is.

CHAPTER 13

KNOCK UNTIL YOU ARE ASTONISHED

Knocking is the last step in this ASK prayer methodology, and it's usually the step that takes the longest amount of time. So long sometimes that we can be surprised when the door opens. It's one thing to keep an ASK note card taped to the mirror for thirty or ninety days, but what about when the prayer request stretches into years? Maybe the note cards have become watermarked from too many toothbrush splashes to the mirror. These are the prayers we are talking about when we think about knocking at the door so long that when it finally opens, we are astonished.

Too Surprised to Open the Door

There is a story in Scripture where Peter knocks on a door and is left standing there because the person on the other side is so astonished to see him! But before we hear about this unopened door, we need a little backstory on what was happening prior to Peter knocking in Acts 12.

King Herod had arrested some followers of Jesus, intending to put them to death. He had already killed James, the brother of John, by piercing him with a sword. Seeing that this pleased the Jews, he arranged to seize Peter. He had him put in prison and surrounded by four squads of four guards each—sixteen soldiers. Peter was in prison, but the church kept praying for him. The night before

Sometimes we can become so weary with the asking, seeking, and knocking that when the door is opened, we forget it's what we've been waiting on forever.

Peter was to be brought to trial, he was sleeping between two soldiers, bound in chains, with sentries on guard at the prison entrance. Suddenly an angel of the Lord appeared with a light in the cell. He struck Peter on the side and said, "Quick, get up!" (v. 7), and the chains fell off Peter's wrists. The angel told Peter to put on his clothes, sandals, and cloak and follow him out of the jail. I love these details because of course the angel would tell Peter to get dressed. Our God is always personal!

After Peter follows the angel past the guards and the iron gates and down the street, he begins to think this is more than a vision or a dream.

As Peter realizes that he has indeed been set free, he goes immediately to the house of Mary, the mother of John Mark, where people were gathered praying. What happens next is so funny!

> Peter knocked at the outer entrance, and a servant named Rhoda came to answer the door. When she recognized Peter's voice, she was so overjoyed she ran back without opening it and exclaimed, "Peter is at the door!"
>
> "You're out of your mind," they told her. When she kept insisting that it was so, they said, "It must be his angel." (vv. 13–15)

The church was gathered to pray for the release of their fellow believers, and when one of them came to the door, the servant Rhoda was too surprised to open the door! Sometimes we can become so weary with the asking, seeking, and knocking that when the door is opened, we are like the church gathered to pray for Peter's release. Overjoyed at the answered prayer but so astonished that God really answered it that we forget it's what we've been waiting on forever.

My Time as Rhoda

I can remember at least one ask where God's answer astonished me. When we moved to Charleston, I left many close friends and family members behind in Charlotte. Even though we felt God's hand on our move, the lack of friends in a new city was hard. This is especially the case for women when moving to a new city because our first focus is getting everyone else settled—the home, the family—and making sure that everyone has what they need in a new place. Moving at the age of forty-six was even tougher for me because most people already had lifelong friends. We had one daughter still in public school, so that helped us link up with other families through Girl Scouts, church groups, and PTAs. But the ache for a girlfriend in my same life stage was real. So real that Gibson prayed for God to bring a special friend into my life. He mentioned it in year two of our relocation, but I didn't think much more about it.

We continued to get plugged in to a new church, serving as small group leaders in men's and women's ministries. About four years after we moved, I decided to go on my first mission trip to Panama with the women's ministry team. I knew only the women's pastor but trusted this would be a great way to get to know other women in the church. There were eight of us on the trip, and when we arrived in Panama, we were assigned roommates by the pastor. I was paired with Kay Sumner, a beautifully cheerful woman my age. The first night, we stayed up until the wee hours of the morning finding out that we had so much in common! Little things, like clip earrings and coffee, and bigger things, like our love for family and traditions.

Kay and I became instant friends and have remained best friends ever since. We make an effort to have lunch or coffee weekly ever since that first mission trip eighteen years ago. It wasn't until about a year into our friendship that my hubby said, "Well, you know I prayed for you to find a best friend. So I'm taking credit for Kay!" Surprised like Rhoda, I hadn't immediately seen God's hand in how He opened a door I thought was closed. As the years have unfolded more unique aspects of our friendship, Kay has also become an accountability partner. She challenges me in areas where I might be forgetting to look to God for answers, and she teaches me continually what it means to love God with all my heart, mind, and soul. One of our favorite sayings is, "A friend is someone who knows the song in your heart and can sing it back to you when you have forgotten the words."

I am thankful every day that my husband knocked for four years with his prayer for a new friend for me.

Skeptical of the Supernatural

There is another lesson in this story about Peter knocking. It's understandable that the servant Rhoda was surprised to find Peter knocking at the door. But what about the very people who were gathered to pray for Peter's release? We find this interesting tidbit about their response: "'You're out of your mind,' they told her. When she kept insisting that it was so, they said, 'It must be his angel'" (Acts 12:15).

Really? The same people who were praying for Peter to be released from prison denied that it could be true when he was standing outside their door. They explained it away as a vision of an angel instead of believing that God could've broken Peter free from his chains.

Have you ever thought for a minute God answered your prayer, but when sharing the results, someone else dismissed it? This age of information we live in is great for instant weather forecasts and up-to-the-minute news feeds. But sometimes too much information makes all of us skeptical of the supernatural. If we can't explain it with a Google search, then it must not be true.

What if the men and women of faith in the Bible dismissed all the times God answered their prayers? I am sure Abraham had a few questions about finding a ram in the bush as a substitute when he was about to sacrifice his son Isaac (see Genesis 22). Can't you imagine how many people thought he was crazy? I can almost hear his wife, Sarah, on his return down the mountain saying, "Well, I'm sure there was a ram in the bush, Abe . . . but let's talk about the voice you heard saying you were supposed to kill our son!" I've heard present-day scientific theories about the parting of the Red Sea or the star of Bethlehem. I'm grateful these scientists weren't around during biblical times to try to debunk the testimonies of God moving and speaking, so that we can have these testimonies as anchors for our faith.

Feet of Faith

Maybe it's not just the information age or scientific answers getting in the way of us having more testimonies about God. Instead, it could be our biblical ancestors were anchored more in their faith in God. They asked; He answered. They sought God's wisdom; He spoke. They knocked on doors with faith; God opened the doors. What if our knocking was anchored in the same faith as Abraham's?

Maybe the difference is in our posture of faith and not that God no longer answers prayer in the same miraculous proportion that we read about in the Bible. It's easy to become discouraged when we're praying what we know to be in the will of God with no obvious answer. I confess that there's one ASK I have been praying for many years with no obvious answer from God. My journals are filled with this prayer. Over the years, my wording of this request has moved from pleading to bargaining to finally a place of trust. My posture of praying in this season of knocking has become "God, I trust You and I believe You are working!" I trust God will answer in what He has determined to be the right time. I highly doubt I'll be surprised like

Rhoda when God answers this prayer because I've written it down in so many prayer journals.

Do you have a prayer like mine that hasn't been answered immediately? Are you continuing to knock until an answer comes? Make sure to capture in writing what you've prayed specifically so you won't dismiss God's answer in your surprise.

Turning Surprise into Awe

My favorite part of the story of Peter knocking happens after Rhoda finally opened the door to Peter. The people gathered to pray weren't sure how to process what was happening, but Peter's passion turned their surprise into shock and awe:

> But Peter kept on knocking, and when they opened the door and saw him, they were astonished. Peter motioned with his hand for them to be quiet and described how the Lord had brought him out of prison. "Tell James and the other brothers and sisters about this," he said, and then he left for another place. (Acts 12:16–17)

Peter basically told them to hush! Then he described what God had done while it was still fresh in his memory. He obviously knew the threat to his life was still valid as he was in a hurry to leave for a new hiding place. Before he left, he shared what God had done and asked them to share it as well with the other brothers and sisters. Peter had experienced the supernatural. As one who had seen the chains broken off his wrists, he didn't have questions or concerns. He had a testimony.

Let us be more like Peter than the people who were praying for Peter. Let our confidence and faith in God, even when we've been knocking for years about the same prayer, turn the response of others from surprise into awe.

ASK in Your Life

1. When have you been like the servant Rhoda and been so surprised at an answer to prayer that you didn't open the door?
   How does this story in Acts 12 give you insight about being
   surprised when God answers?

2. Maybe you've shared an answered prayer and well-intentioned
   friends dismissed it as luck or timing. How can you keep from
   being discouraged when others don't understand your answer?
   Read more about Abraham in Genesis 22 to encourage you in
   your knocking.

3. How could writing your prayers and journaling God's specific
   answers help you feel more confident in long times of knocking
   in prayer?

CHAPTER 14

KNOCKING SOMETIMES HURTS

There may be times in your prayer life, in the ask, seek, and knock process, when your prayers haven't yet been answered and a sense of defeat settles in. This is one of the most discouraging times because that defeat can turn into questioning—or, worse, self-doubt. Self-doubt can hurt us emotionally, mentally, or spiritually if we allow the knocking to turn everything inward instead of upward. There were many times during my single-mom years when the pain of my past caused me to doubt my choices and ultimately my worthiness to keep asking and keep knocking. Doubting our worth as a child of God is one of the most painful places to be because we are relying on our own strength and power instead of trusting in God. This leads to a despair and loneliness more painful than rapping our knuckles on a door for hours on end.

Hurting in the Garden

While I didn't have any self-worth books or podcasts during my single-again days, I did have my Bible, and I turned to it often during those years. One of the most poignant stories in the Bible of knocking until it hurts is just before the crucifixion on the night when Jesus was in the garden of Gethsemane. Though Jesus didn't doubt His identity as God's Son, I still resonated with the pain and loneliness He felt in His unanswered prayers:

> Then Jesus went with his disciples to a place called Gethsemane, and he said to them, "Sit here while I go over there and pray." He took Peter and the two sons of Zebedee along with him, and he began to be sorrowful and troubled. Then he said to them, "My soul is overwhelmed with sorrow to the point of death. Stay here and keep watch with me."
>
> Going a little farther, he fell with his face to the ground and prayed, "My Father, if it is possible, may this cup be taken from me. Yet not as I will, but as you will."
>
> Then he returned to his disciples and found them sleeping. "Couldn't you men keep watch with me for one hour?" he asked Peter. "Watch and pray so that you will not fall into temptation. The spirit is willing, but the flesh is weak." (Matthew 26:36–41)

Jesus knew the end was near. He brought his three closest disciples with Him, telling them His soul was deeply grieved to the point of death. He asked them to stay and keep watch, but they fell asleep! In their defense, John Gill's *Exposition of the Bible* reminds us that they had just made great preparations for the Passover feast and then eaten a huge meal, so sleep was not surprising. He also suggests that maybe Satan induced their sleep.[13] Whether it was the lamb or the Enemy, the effect of their sleeping instead of keeping watch and praying was that Jesus realized He was alone. That sense of loneliness remained when He went away again and they disappointed Him once more:

> He went away a second time and prayed, "My Father, if it is not possible for this cup to be taken away unless I drink it, may your will be done."

146

When he came back, he again found them sleeping, because their eyes were heavy. So he left them and went away once more and prayed the third time, saying the same thing.

Then he returned to the disciples and said to them, "Are you still sleeping and resting? Look, the hour has come, and the Son of Man is delivered into the hands of sinners. Rise! Let us go! Here comes my betrayer!" (vv. 42–46)

With the language of betrayal, Jesus shifts from speaking about "you men" to a singular "my." Jesus had traveled, taught, laughed, and cried with the Twelve for the past three years, but suddenly He realized He was alone in what was coming next.

Loneliness hurts like no other hurt.

If Jesus felt betrayal and loneliness during His greatest hour of prayer, we are even more likely to fall into this same pit of loneliness during times of need.

Connection Defeats Loneliness

Jesus was the Son of God, and if Jesus felt betrayal and loneliness during His greatest hour of prayer, we are even more likely to fall into this same pit of loneliness during times of need. It's at this point in knocking when we should phone a friend or ask someone to join in the praying.

Solomon, the writer of Ecclesiastes, knew this when he wrote,

Two are better than one,
    because they have a good return for their labor:
if either of them falls down,
    one can help the other up.
But pity anyone who falls
    and has no one to help them up.
Also, if two lie down together, they will keep warm.

But how can one keep warm alone?
Though one may be overpowered,
   two can defend themselves.
A cord of three strands is not quickly broken. (4:9–12)

A "cord of three strands" refers to rope, and when three strands are braided together, the cord is stronger and not easily torn apart. The teaching here is obvious since the previous verses refer to "two are better than one" with people. Also, when we ask someone else to pray with us, pride is defeated and replaced with humility. It's difficult to maintain a stance of independence or self-reliance when you confess needs with a partner in prayer. If we take this passage from Ecclesiastes and apply it to knocking in prayer, the words might look like this:

> Two are better than one when praying, for together they will receive comfort through community while they are knocking. If one of them becomes discouraged, the other one will lift up their spirit!
>
> Woe to the one who falls to loneliness because of self-reliance. The prayers of two will have more Holy Spirit fire than one! One can be overcome by the Enemy when praying, but two can resist him. A strand of three, two people plus the Holy Spirit, is indestructible!

While it seems logical to reach out to someone when we're hurting, it's often the last thing we want to do. During my single-again days, I felt as if the rest of the world were married. Certainly on the surface it can feel as if we're alone in our pain. As I review some of my journals from those years, this entry was painfully poetic of those days and nights:

> It is Friday night and because Friday nights have become difficult for me in the past few years, it is appropriate that I share these feelings. While married, Friday nights were always Family Nights going out to dinner with my parents

and then playing spades or hearts at their home. Later it became ball games or events with the whole family. Now as a single parent working a non-career job all week, I hit Friday nights like the coyote hit the brick wall while chasing the roadrunner. Full of expectation and hope yet crashing into the reality of exhaustion and loneliness.

I am ever grateful for couples and families who didn't let me sit in my loneliness but instead provided community and connection. Their friendship allowed me to move from isolation and self-doubt to wholeness and eventually trusting God to answer my prayers. One couple, Kay and Del Smith, invited me and my daughters over for dinner many times. Or if the girls were busy, they invited me alone. I did not need a spouse or date to be complete, and the three of us were a strong triple-braided cord! Another family, Karen and Terry Gray, included me in their family Christmas Day celebration the first year I was alone. I will never forget the inclusive love I experienced from these families as they stretched the boundaries of their family units to include one that looked a little different.

Are you in a season of isolation that has kept you looking inward instead of upward to God? Find a group or connect with other believers while you wait for answers to your prayers.

Refocusing Our Prayers

Sometimes when we've been knocking until it hurts, it's time to focus on something besides the pain. Without giving up on our ask, seek, and knock prayers, simply refocusing our thoughts and prayers can be just what we need to break the cycle of defeat, loneliness, and despair. How to refocus? The easiest way is to practice gratitude. Thankfully, God was teaching me this truth soon after my whiny journal entry about my lonely Friday nights. My next entry was written on New Year's Day in a new journal given to me by my daughter Katie:

Thank you for Katie and Jessie. They bring me so much joy, it sometimes overflows my heart. Jessie is learning to read and so eager to prove herself—she read "Sally, Dick and Jane" four times tonight! Bless her free spirit and warm hugs! Katie drew up a contract with herself to become more organized. Bless her independence! Thank you, Lord, for the fullness of my life. My only prayer is that I don't abuse any of your gifts! Love, Debbie.

What a change in focus! I went from hitting the wall of exhaustion and loneliness to proclaiming gratitude over the fullness of my life. My single status wouldn't change for four more years, but this shift toward gratitude certainly affected the way I reflect upon those years. Many of my ASK prayers were still in the knocking stage, but by turning toward gratitude, the knocking was no longer painful. Besides praying for a spouse and remarriage, I was also knocking for many years in ASKs related to financial freedom, serving God in full-time ministry, a home for our family, and health for extended family members. But when I looked up and became thankful, I recognized who God is and acknowledged His power. One Scripture passage even teaches us to practice gratitude in our praying: "Do not be anxious about anything, but in every situation, by prayer and petition, with thanksgiving, present your requests to God. And the peace of God, which transcends all understanding, will guard your hearts and your minds in Christ Jesus" (Philippians 4:6–7).

We often focus on the first phrase in that passage, "Do not be anxious about anything," when in fact Paul is reminding us to present all our requests with thanksgiving (or gratitude). I know that God was teaching me through this passage during my single-again years because the verses that follow were printed out and taped to the inside cover of the leather planner I carried to work: "Finally, brothers and sisters, whatever is true, whatever is noble, whatever is right, whatever is pure, whatever is lovely, whatever is admirable—if anything is excellent or praiseworthy—think about such things. Whatever you have learned or received or heard from me, or seen in me—put it into practice. And the God of peace will be with you" (vv. 8–9).

Sometimes it's necessary to speak to our soul and remind our spirit how to think and pray. It was true for me then, and it's a good reminder for any time we become weary in our prayers to the point of hurting.

The Epidural for Prayer

The truth is that ask, seek, and knock is a great formula that Jesus gave us in Matthew 7:7 for praying, but there's no guarantee that the process will be pain-free. Prayer is like childbirth: sometimes it includes long labor and delivery pains, while other times a caesarean section might bypass the labor but still causes pain and entails a longer recovery. During some of my ASK prayers, I have endured long months or years of knocking and painful labor along the way. Others have had shorter times of knocking with some recovery after. Either way, there is pain involved.

If you've ever had a long labor before childbirth, you know the blessing of an epidural shot. My first delivery with Katie lasted twenty-eight hours, and I didn't receive the first epidural until my sister-in-law convinced me at the halfway point that it could still be a natural birth. The relief from my back labor was so immediate and sweet, I remember saying, "Why didn't someone give me this shot during my ninth month of pregnancy?"

Jesus's example from the garden of Gethsemane shows us the pain of betrayal, loneliness, and despair He felt while praying. If Jesus, the Son of God, felt these emotions, that gives me assurance that I'm not alone when experiencing the same feelings when I pray. More importantly, He was teaching us that to push through the pain of knocking, we must release our will. Twice in this garden prayer, Jesus said, "Not as I will, but as you will" (Matthew 26:39; see also v. 42).

Sometimes when I've been praying and knocking, my hand is also on the doorknob, trying to force it open. Only when I release my hand, and my will, does the knocking cease to hurt. Similar to the physical pain we might encounter when trying to force open a closed or locked door, we experience pain trying to force our way to an answer to prayer. While Jesus still encountered the pain of dying on a cross, the release of His will in the garden allowed Him to walk that path freely. We see this in three instances immediately following His prayer to release His will in the garden:

- He rose from praying and said: "Look, the hour has come, and the Son of Man is delivered into the hands of sinners. Rise! Let us go! Here comes my betrayer!" (vv. 45–46).
- Jesus allowed Judas to betray Him: "Going at once to Jesus, Judas said, 'Greetings, Rabbi!' and kissed him. Jesus replied, 'Do what you came for, friend'" (vv. 49–50).
- As a disciple responded with a sword, Jesus taught them to respond in love: "Jesus said to the crowd, 'Am I leading a rebellion, that you have come out with swords and clubs to capture me? Every day I sat in the temple courts teaching, and you did not arrest me. But this has all taken place that the writings of the prophets might be fulfilled" (vv. 55–56).

Now I think about releasing my will during prayer much like an epidural. If I can remember to knock like Jesus did in the garden, I will have less pain because I will be able to release my hand from trying to push the door open. Then I can proceed in love and freedom—even if the answer takes much longer than I hoped.

ASK in Your Life

1. Connection helps us overcome loneliness and self-defeat while knocking in prayer. How can you apply the truths in Ecclesiastes 4:9–12? Perhaps you can phone a friend to ask them to partner with you in prayer.

2 Perhaps you're in a secure place with God, and He's prompting you to reach out to someone who needs connection. Who has God brought into your circles who might need a shared dinner or to be included in your family's next gathering?

3. Since shifting to gratitude helps us defeat despair when in a long season of knocking, try starting or restarting a gratitude journal. Name three things every day you're grateful for and thank God for each one.

4. In which area of prayer is your hand on the doorknob, gently or strongly nudging it open? Study Jesus's example in the garden of Gethsemane (Matthew 26) and see what surrender looks like, then apply it to your personal knocking.

CHAPTER 15

KEEP ON KNOCKING

Have you been praying for something or someone for so many years that it feels hopeless? Usually when one of my ASKs for a specific thing or change in my life is not answered, I'll shift the ASK over time as I align it more with God's will. When praying for someone else—and unable to shift that person's circumstances—it can be tempting to give up. Maybe you've been praying for a child or a friend with an addiction. There's no doubt that it's God's will for them to be free of addiction. Or maybe you're praying for a parent to experience financial freedom. It's certainly God's will that no one would be in bondage to debt. Or maybe you have prayed—as I have—that a loved one would come to a personal knowledge and acceptance of Jesus as their Savior. In each of these scenarios, we know that He wants every person to experience the fullness of life described here: "The thief comes only to steal and kill and destroy. I came that they may have life and have it abundantly" (John 10:10 ESV).

In intercessory prayer is where the long game of knocking comes into play. Especially when we're praying for others, it may sometimes take years or decades to see God's answers. We need great tenacity in praying these ASKs, a dogged persistence to keep on knocking until the door is opened.

Always Means Always

When I am discouraged by seemingly hopeless ASKs, I find great encouragement in the story we often call the parable of the persistent widow, found in Luke:

> And he told them a parable to the effect that they ought always to pray and not lose heart. He said, "In a certain city there was a judge who neither feared God nor respected man. And there was a widow in that city who kept coming to him and saying, 'Give me justice against my adversary.' For a while he refused, but afterward he said to himself, 'Though I neither fear God nor respect man, yet because this widow keeps bothering me, I will give her justice, so that she will not beat me down by her continual coming.'" And the Lord said, "Hear what the unrighteous judge says. And will not God give justice to his elect, who cry to him day and night? Will he delay long over them? I tell you, he will give justice to them speedily. Nevertheless, when the Son of Man comes, will he find faith on earth?" (18:1–8 ESV)

I did some digging into the Greek words in this passage and found the following:

- "They ought *always* to pray"—the Greek is *pantote*, meaning "at all times, forevermore."
- "Justice to his *elect*"—the Greek is *eklektos*, meaning "people who choose to follow the Lord."

What does this look at the original language of the passage tell us? First, we are to always pray, and *always* means "at all times, forevermore." Not until we are weary. Not until we think the ASK is unanswerable. Not until we've given up on mankind. No! *Forevermore* is a stronger word than *persistent*. Persistence can run dry, depending on our emotional state or whether we've got the right vitamins in our body. If we read the passage to say that we should pray like the widow—forevermore—that is a lot clearer.

Also, it was not just that the widow prayed forevermore but that she is described as one of the "elect," a chosen one who has deep faith. If there was ever a mentor to emulate, she is it. At the end of my days and the end of my praying, I want to be known as a chosen one with deep faith. Don't you? I don't want my epitaph to read, "She prayed until she gave up," or "She was almost one of God's chosen."

Keep On Keepin' On

There have been times when I've been knocking in the right way but not at the right time or place. That's when I've found it is critical to just keep on knocking.

One of these times was when I felt called to work full-time in ministry. We'd been attending and serving at a megachurch for six years, and I had also become friends with many of the staff. My past volunteer experience, business career, and online seminary training suited me to work in an organization of this size, so I browsed their job openings. The first position I applied for was bookstore manager. I loved reading, and bookstores of any kind were a favorite hangout. I had years of experience in retailing, so this seemed a good match. I applied and sent in my résumé but never got an interview. No call. No email. Just a rejection letter. I was asking, seeking, and knocking, so I decided to wait for the next available position to be posted online. This one was for the online campus pastor. Perfect, I thought, as I imagined myself in this position. I had begun a blog and embraced all things technology related, keeping up to date through my younger daughters. Again, a rejection letter without a call or interview. I think there was a third position I applied for, but I can't remember what it was. I must've felt so defeated that I've blocked the memory.

Six months passed, and I began to believe that the calling into full-time ministry was my own invention or a desire that wouldn't be realized. Then our women's pastor called and asked me to lunch one day. Over lunch, Pastor Betsy Smith told me that she had an opening for an assistant, and though she knew I was overqualified, she felt the nudge from God to have me apply. After praying about it with my husband, we knew this was my open door from all the many years of knocking. Beginning as Pastor Betsy's assistant was the best place for me to learn women's ministry from the first steps of connection to discipling coaches. God knew exactly which door to open for me. A couple of years later when she retired, I was positioned with experience to lead women's ministry and become a pastor to women.

> **Whether we get tired of knocking or pride keeps us from trying another door, God never leaves us in the process.**

Sometimes we are knocking on the wrong door, but in His mercy, God allows us to keep knocking until we knock at the door He designed us to walk through.

Whether we get tired of knocking or pride keeps us from trying another door, God never leaves us in the process. The title to a popular song by Curtis Mayfield comes to mind as encouragement: "Keep On Keeping On."

Knocking in God's Perfect Timing

The other important part about my knocking on doors for a career in full-time ministry was that when the door was finally opened by our women's pastor, it was God opening the door and not me forcing it open.

A friend of mine often reminds me that when knocking on a door, we should do everything possible to walk through it without breaking the door down. Easier said than done, right? Everything in our culture today tells us that we make our own destiny. We are in control of our future. We need to take the reins for our own success. Wait a minute! Did God say any of that?

Jesus was continually telling His followers that they didn't have the full picture or understand the perfect timing behind His actions. One of my favorite examples of this is in the story of Lazarus's death in John 11:1–44.

Lazarus and his sisters, Martha and Mary, lived in Bethany, and Lazarus had fallen sick. They sent word to Jesus to come. Jesus knew and loved this family well, but when He heard Lazarus was sick, He said, "This sickness will not end in death. No, it is for God's glory so that God's Son may be glorified through it" (v. 4).

Jesus stayed where he was for two more days and then told the disciples they should go to Bethany: "Our friend Lazarus has fallen asleep; but I am going there to wake him up" (v. 11). This caused more confusion, as the disciples tried to convince Jesus that maybe Lazarus needed more sleep.

Whew. That sounds a lot like me whenever one of my daughters is struggling emotionally or physically. They know my sure response is usually, "Maybe you need a shower or a nap." But Jesus was speaking of Lazarus's death and how He would be waking him up from the dead, yet the disciples didn't understand.

They went on the journey to Lazarus's tomb and watched Jesus weep with Mary and Martha over their brother. Then Jesus commanded the stone in front of the tomb to be rolled back and said, "Lazarus, come out!" (v. 43)—and once-dead Lazarus walked out of the tomb with all his grave clothes.

Martha was worried about the stench since her brother had been dead so long. She thought it was too late for Jesus to heal Lazarus. But Jesus was about to perform the biggest death-to-life miracle ever witnessed to this point in time, and no one got it. Not even the disciples who had been under His personal teaching for almost three years.

I am actually encouraged by their dullness, since it gives me grace for all the times I don't understand God's timing or continue to wait on doors to open. We see what seem to be our next steps—we ask, do a little seeking, and then knock. Then those cultural lies of "make your own destiny" creep back in whenever the waiting period is too long.

Maybe you know in your head that God's timing is perfect, but still you've been like me and kicked a few doors down. Maybe you've been discouraged with knocking for the same prayer with the same faithfulness, and logic overrules your spirit. What do we do when the knocking has gone on so long that our faith is depleted and we want to give up?

Remember Who He Is

I was recently asked what I do when I'm waiting for an answer to prayer and my faith is running dry, and my first and only answer was: "I have to remember who God is." When I'm losing faith or weary with the knocking, there's only one place to look for answers, and that's in the Bible. God's Word reminds me of His character. His promises remind me that He will never leave me or turn me away. His stories of redemption remind me that if He did something for His people in ages past, He will do something for me. His instruction about waiting reminds me that I don't have the full picture or the perfect timing. Several Scripture verses on waiting are good ones to keep handy, because we will become weary and we will become discouraged. If we read these promises over ourselves and speak courage into our spirits, we will remember who He is. I'll close this section with a few of my favorites that I keep at the front of every journal and readily available on my phone:

> Let us not become weary in doing good, for at the proper time we will reap a harvest if we do not give up. (Galatians 6:9)

> Trust in the LORD with all your heart
> and lean not on your own understanding;
> in all your ways submit to him,
> and he will make your paths straight. (Proverbs 3:5–6)

But those who hope in the LORD
  will renew their strength.
They will soar on wings like eagles;
    they will run and not grow weary,
    they will walk and not be faint. (Isaiah 40:31)

Blessed is the one who perseveres under trial because, having stood the test, that person will receive the crown of life that the Lord has promised to those who love him. (James 1:12)

ASK in Your Life

1. Study the story of the persistent widow in Luke 18:1–8. How does knowing the Greek meaning of the phrase translated "they ought always to pray" encourage you to keep knocking? What other portions of this Scripture can you apply personally?

2. Where has pride gotten in the way so you haven't kept on knocking? Confess your pride and move forward toward asking and believing as you continue praying.

3. In what ways do you relate to Martha in the story of Lazarus's death? When was a time that you didn't see the long view of what God was doing? Maybe you're in that season now. Read John 11 to remember that His delays are always purposeful if we keep knocking.

4. If you've been losing faith due to unanswered prayers, how can you focus instead on the qualities of God? Write down or memorize these Scriptures to remind you of who God is: Exodus 3:13–14, Psalm 116:5, Isaiah 40:28, 1 Corinthians 10:13, 1 Timothy 1:17, 1 John 4:7–9.

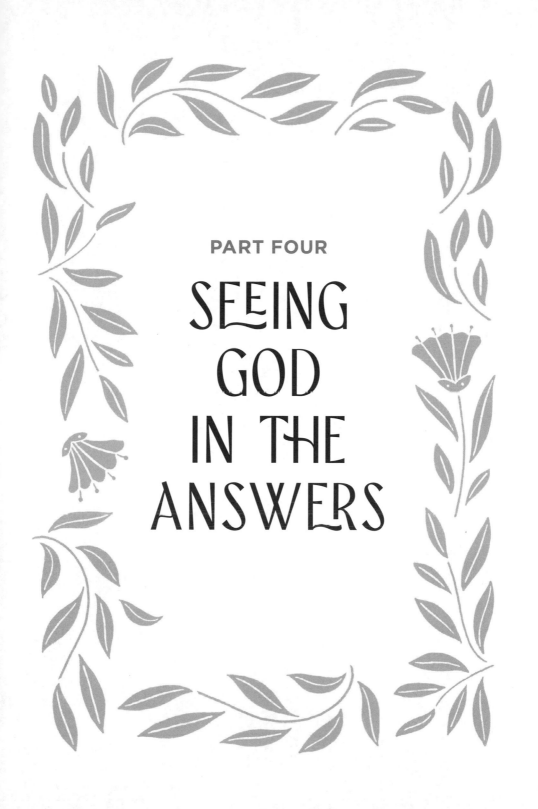

PART FOUR

SEEING GOD IN THE ANSWERS

CHAPTER 16

TRUSTING WITH A YES, NO, OR NOT NOW

Before writing this book, I was curious to find out what keeps people from praying. So I put together a survey on social media and found the responses broke down into three categories:

1. People don't know how to pray, or they think it's too complicated.
2. People don't have time to pray, or they get distracted.
3. People don't think God answers prayers.

Hopefully, the previous sections on asking, seeking, and knocking have helped you if you found yourself in camp one or two. And even though those who responded with number three were only 14 percent, they might have been the bravest and the most vulnerable. Because if we're honest, I think most of us dip our toe into the water of disbelief at times. When I think about my own seasons of life when prayer became a struggle or was not my default, it was because very few people had written about how to see God in answered prayers. So let's pull back the curtain on some different ways that God does answer our asks.

Not all answers to prayer are "yes." It's nice when they are, but just as often God will answer us with a "no" or "not now." Being able to discern a yes, a no, or a not now is important because then we are able to move on instead of becoming stuck waiting for our yes. More importantly, knowing that God is answering us even when it's a no elevates Him to the status He deserves and reminds us He is not a genie in a bottle. In order for us to not lose hope, it's vital that we also see "not now," or delayed answers, as answers still. We are short-minded humans with the prayer attention span of handling about one crisis at a time. When we're watching and taking notes, it's easier to see delayed answers to questions we might have stopped asking.

A No Could Lead to a Better Answer

When we pray an ask and get a hard no, it's easy to slip into believing that God isn't for us. We're asking what seems to be in His will and for our best life. But there are times when our ask has a limited viewpoint, namely our own. We don't see from a kingdom perspective or even have the vision to ask for what is really God's best. An example we have of a hard no in the Bible is when Abraham was talking with God about making Ishmael his heir in Genesis:

> God also said to Abraham, "As for Sarai your wife, you are no longer to call her Sarai; her name will be Sarah. I will bless her and will surely give you a son by her. I will bless her so that she will be the mother of nations; kings of peoples will come from her."
>   Abraham fell facedown; he laughed and said to himself, "Will a son be born to a man a hundred years old? Will Sarah bear a child at the age of ninety?" And Abraham said to God, "If only Ishmael might live under your blessing!" (17:15–18)

God had already told Abraham that Sarah would give him a son, but due to their ages, he didn't believe it. Abraham asked if his son Ishmael might be his heir instead. But in the next verses, God said no:

Then God said, "Yes, but your wife Sarah will bear you a son, and you will call him Isaac. I will establish my covenant with him as an everlasting covenant for his descendants after him. And as for Ishmael, I have heard you: I will surely bless him; I will make him fruitful and will greatly increase his numbers. He will be the father of twelve rulers, and I will make him into a great nation." (vv. 19–20)

We simply don't understand God's ways or His ability to do the miraculous in our lives, do we? By continually putting Him on the same level as humanity, we wonder why our prayers are sometimes answered with a no. God gave us this story to remember His ways are better, even when we can't see them.

When a No Leads to a Best Yes

Sometimes in our ASKs, there are multiple ways we can move forward. The most recent time I had this kind of ASK on the table with God was in the process of this book being published. God had already confirmed an agent to represent *Simply Pray*, but as a new author, I learned there are quite a few steps in shopping your work to various publishers.

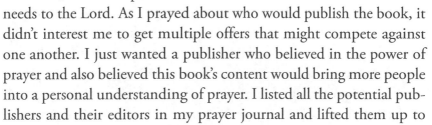

It can be easy for us to get discouraged with a no, but if we trust that God is directing our path, then we won't receive it as a rejection but as a redirection.

My list of needs in a publisher was short, and I had presented those needs to the Lord. As I prayed about who would publish the book, it didn't interest me to get multiple offers that might compete against one another. I just wanted a publisher who believed in the power of prayer and also believed this book's content would bring more people into a personal understanding of prayer. I listed all the potential publishers and their editors in my prayer journal and lifted them up to

God on a weekly basis. Each time my agent, Tom Dean, sent me an email with a no from one of those publishers, I replied, "That no will just lead to the best yes." Those weren't empty words but a daily releasing of control of every step to feel God's peace in the process. It can be easy for us to get discouraged with a no, but if we trust that God is directing our path, then we won't receive it as a rejection but as a redirection.

A No Could Mean Not Now

One time God answered me with a not now was when I thought He was calling me into corporate chaplaincy (see chapter 9). It felt like a path that was confirmed in all the right ways. But at the end of my certification, there were no chaplaincy positions in our new city of Charleston. Fast-forward ten years to when I was serving in women's ministry and taking courses that would lead to ordination. When the ordination pastor discovered I'd taken one year of courses for chaplaincy and one year of online seminary, my credits were filled! With some training for ceremonies and pastoral counseling, I was ordained as a pastor. God knew exactly which courses I needed for my future roles, and He used each portion of those studies to give me the knowledge and understanding needed for a call in the future. Why do we sometimes think a delay means no?

Not only was this a ten-year delay from when I took the courses, but it was closer to a forty-year delay from when I first felt God calling me into ministry. As a teenager experiencing new life in Christ after my salvation, I also was beginning to feel a love for the church. This happened while I was exploring colleges, so I included seminary in my areas of interest. Unfortunately, this was during the seventies when women were not readily accepted into seminary, and my pastor at the time was quick to confirm this. He told me that I could pursue children's ministry or music ministry, but women didn't pursue teaching or preaching in seminary.

Well, I wasn't good enough in music to lead others, and I didn't think I liked children enough to teach them. The seventies were also a time when many young people were getting degrees in psychology and sociology but were unable to find jobs. My father wisely guided me into business administration and accounting—more employable skills. Thus began my career in the corporate world, first as a buyer and later in administrative management. During all those years, I was quietly yearning to be in full-time ministry. Not only yearning, I felt unfulfilled. Many times I questioned whether God had heard my prayers as a fifteen-year-old or, later, thirty-five-year-old. It seemed as if my prayers were humble and positioned to glorify Him, certainly not to make a better salary or a name for myself. I often wondered why God didn't answer my prayers or if He heard them at all. To be honest, many times I believed it was because I wasn't worthy of such a calling. I never thought that it might be because He was doing something in the process to lead to His ultimate goal for me.

Work in Process

Do you feel as if you're on a path that isn't leading to your ultimate dream? Maybe as in my example, your prayer for that eventual placement is being answered with a delay while you receive the training you will need. Or maybe you have a no in another type of ask, and God sees other scenarios at work that will lead to a better yes. It's so hard to see the work in process sometimes because we're striving for the end goal.

Let's look at an example close to my heart. A few ago I became passionate about peonies. I'm not sure where these exotic flowers had been all my life, but I became obsessed with growing them and having them for vases of cut flowers. Step one of my plan to grow peonies involved research and vision. After online research telling me they would grow in my zone, local experts begged to differ. Many local horticulturalists told me that peonies don't thrive in the low country, and they each had stories to confirm those hard facts. A few were still encouraging, telling me to give it my best shot and report back if successful.

It seemed as if I wasn't the only gardener obsessed with peonies. I ordered the bare roots from a reputable nursery that shipped them on the exact week they should be planted in our zone. The root bulbs were planted with care and the prescribed fertilizers in time for the last cold freeze of winter, which helps them grow. I planted the bulbs in a variety of locations and put a couple in containers, just to ensure success. Then I waited.

At the end of spring, I started to see green sprouts pop up, and I faithfully watered and watched. They continued to shoot up in summer, but no buds or blossoms. It was then that I started to pay attention to an oft-repeated line in my peony research: unlike annuals, peonies take three to four years to become blooming plants. The first year of growth is focused on root production and becoming established in the garden. If blooms occur the first year, they may be smaller and not the typical form or color of mature flowers.

Still, I knew my peonies would be quick producers. Until winter began and the green stems all disappeared. But in year two, at the first onset of spring, the plants sprang up from the ground or pots where I had forgotten they lay dormant. One plant even had a tiny bud, which I quickly snipped and nurtured with warm water to produce a lovely blossom. The plants all looked healthy, but no other blossoms were currently viable.

In your years of waiting, what roots are being established beneath the soil of your prayers?

My years as a buyer taught me to look at trends statistically and to study the market to see what products people liked. Years in administrative management taught me about process improvement, proofreading, budget worksheets, and getting the right person in place for every job. Looking back, each one of those skills learned and refined in a corporate setting helped me in leading a women's ministry of four thousand women. Many times I mined the church databases to see what the demographics were for our women before visioning a new series or conference. Years of submitting and complying with budgets helped me stretch slim portions allocated monthly when ministry activities were sometimes seasonal. Years of proofreading made newsletters easier and even now writing a book less cumbersome. Process improvement? Well, I guess it might make me more efficient at laundry or cooking weekly for our growing family.

Maybe you are a teacher and have a desire to be a speaker. What better root system could you be growing than learning to communicate to sometimes unwilling participants? Or maybe your dream is to start your own business, but right now you are behind a desk and a computer fulfilling customer requests. Hearing from and learning what the customer wants will be crucial to any business you start. It might be that you are a stay-at-home mom with two or more kiddos under the age of five and your days feel like an endless loop of feeding, changing, and caring for these humans. Whatever your future calling, you are learning to put others first, which will serve you well when you have the capacity to serve others.

Waiting for a Yes

I love gardening, and it isn't lost on me that most everything related to this hobby is the result of slow and steady growth. As with the peonies, I am constantly waiting on my lime bush to produce or my perennials to bounce back after a hard freeze. But driven achiever types aren't particularly good at waiting. Right? We like to complete the list, see the finished product, and move on to the next thing.

Why did I take up gardening? There is constantly work to be done with the soil or the roots to ensure they don't get jammed tightly in a space. After last year's unexpected hard freeze in the South, some of my plants died and didn't come back. This setback caused me to rethink some plant choices and placement. Sometimes a transplant is necessary to move a plant for just the right light. In the same way, when we get a no to our asks, it's a good time to evaluate our prayer and see if it lines up with God's will. If it does, we also know that God sees the endgame for us and it's not always visible in today's answers.

This is exactly why gardening is the right hobby for me as I'm reminded of all the work God is doing in process as I relearn the value of waiting. When I review the years of my prayers and how many times God answered "not yet," it reminds me that His beauty comes in the waiting, and His yes is always better than anything I could have asked for.

ASK in Your Life

1. Which of the three answers would you give about why you don't pray more: you don't know how to pray, you don't have time to pray, or you don't think God answers prayers? Did this chapter shift your previous thoughts?

2. In looking back over some no answers you've received to prayers, how can you see now that they might have led to a best yes?

3. What prayer do you have today that could be a work in process? In your years of waiting, what roots are growing beneath the soil of your prayers?

4. Study John 15:1–17 for a look at being pruned and clinging to the Vine (Jesus) while waiting for harvest.

CHAPTER 17

THE ANSWER IS IN THE BOOK

Have you ever had an open-book exam? I can only remember one from my years of college but have recently heard our grandkids talk about them more. At first it sounds like a cinch to get an A on a test when you're allowed to look through the book for your answers, right? But then you look at the size of the textbook and it's a twelve-hundred-page book with fine print, and suddenly an A doesn't seem so easy. What teachers know about these tests is that a student needs to be familiar enough with the book to go to the right section or page quickly in order to find a specific answer. If a student has been in the book daily as the subject is being taught, the material is familiar and answers will be easily found during a test.

Seeing God's answers to our prayers is similar to an open-book test. We have the Bible, God's divine and inspired words, complex and full of mysteries. And if we study it, become familiar with it, and strive to understand it, we can also see it as an instruction book for life, available for any test or situation. A favorite passage of mine reminding us of this is found in Psalm 119:105: "Your word is a lamp to my feet and a light to my path" (ESV).

The Hebrew for "lamp" in this verse is *ner*, which means "a single candlelight," much like the lanterns with candles they wore strapped to their ankles in the psalmists' days. The Hebrew for "light" in "a light to my path" is *owr*, which is more like an illumination. God's Word will show us the next step and the pathway ahead.

An Illuminated Answer

One time God's Word was a specific answer to me and illuminated my path much like a candle. This was during my years serving as a pastor and director of women's ministry when we decided to start an annual women's conference. We gathered a team of ten women to help determine the vision and name for this conference. For several initial meetings, we prayed and talked about the women we were serving and brainstormed names for it. We had adjectives and descriptions covering many whiteboards, but nothing resonated with what we felt our women needed spoken over them. We wanted one word that would affirm, teach, encourage, and propel women into their next steps with God.

That one word seemed elusive until late one evening while I was studying my Bible on the sofa with my daughter Jess. In the back of my mind, I continued to work on the struggle to find a conference name. Suddenly I looked down at my Bible at this verse, and the word jumped off the page: "The Spirit of the Sovereign LORD is upon me, because the LORD has *chosen* me" (Isaiah 61:1 NET, emphasis added).

That was it. God wanted His daughters to know that they were chosen. Jess looked over at my notes and wrote the word in a large script on her journal page with a period after it. Chosen. And so it has been called The Chosen Conference since 2012, teaching and encouraging thousands of women each year and reminding them how precious they are to their heavenly Father.

Maybe you aren't looking for a conference name but are instead praying an ASK and needing God's wisdom. If you're reading the Bible regularly and a word keeps leaping off the page, highlight it and ask God to show you how it applies to your life. As with the word I kept getting from Isaiah 40:31 (in chapter 7), I knew that "waiting on the Lord" was the phrase that applied to our job transitions and eventual move. In our seeking we will find the answers, and sometimes those answers are in the Book.

Some of Us Need a Chapter

Although there have been times when God answered me with a specific Scripture, sometimes we need more. Whenever Christians talk about having a life verse, I usually giggle and say that I'm such a handful, God had to give me a whole chapter.

It was in 1998 when I heard Isaiah 43:18–19 in a sermon and knew that it was for me: "Forget the former things; do not dwell on the past. See, I am doing a new thing!"

It's no surprise that these verses were an answer to my prayers about how to blend our family in the first few years of my new marriage with Gibson. There were so many areas to work through including holidays with three sets of parents, reframing traditions, merging bank accounts, and redefining our family culture. In my dog-eared Bible from those days, I marked *1/98* in the margin beside these verses. Was finding these verses of my own making? Did I just choose something that would fit my situation? No. They resonated deep within me about the new family and new life we were forming together. Whether I heard these verses in church or at a conference, they plunged me deep into studying all of Isaiah 43. I marked and highlighted other verses, and now looking back they almost strategically write my story of that year like a page in my journal:

> 7/98: Do not be afraid, for I am with you; I will bring
> your children from the east and gather you from the west.
> I will say to the north, "Give them up!" And to the south,
> "Do not hold them back." (vv. 5–6)

I don't have any other notes to explain why this passage was so critical to me later that year, but it was during our season of teen rebellion when I was praying about how to parent a prodigal, so it was probably comforting to this mama's heart. It was also important to me in later seasons as our adult daughters traveled and moved to various parts of the country, far from our East Coast home. As I prayed about how to navigate keeping our family connected across the country, verses 5 and 6 reminded me the Lord heard my cries and would keep us tethered.

> 11/98: But now, this is what the LORD says—he who created you, O Jacob, he who formed you, Israel: "Do not fear, for I have redeemed you; I have summoned you by name; you are mine. When you pass through the waters, I will be with you; and when you pass through the rivers, they will not sweep over you. When you walk through the fire, you will not be burned; the flames will not set you ablaze. For I am the LORD your God, the Holy One of Israel, your Savior." (vv. 1–3)

These verses right at the beginning of chapter 43 are often quoted, written about, and spoken. They are powerful words for each one of us, and if I had to choose one portion of the chapter as mine, it would be this: Created. Formed. Redeemed. Summoned. His. Safe.

Context Brings Understanding

God was so mercifully personal to give me Isaiah 43 when I needed a lifeline. That single chapter was all I understood of any of the history of the book of Isaiah or its context within the whole Bible. But He didn't need me to be a theologian or have complete understanding to give me this daily bread. God is so good that way: giving us what we need when we need it. But a few years later, I was able to take a yearlong study with others at our church that brought new meaning to every verse and chapter in Scripture. In this in-depth study of the Bible from Genesis to Revelation, using *Disciple: Becoming Disciples through Bible Study* by Richard and Julia Wilke, we learned to read the Bible not as many books with many authors but as one book with just One divine author.

This study taught us about literary themes in the books of the Bible, human depravity, and God's great rescue. But the most important thing I learned during this study over twenty-five years ago was the thread of covenant that runs from Genesis to Revelation. When I saw this thread pulled from Abraham to Jesus, it gave a more profound meaning to every step of my journey with God. The implications of my covenant with God—and His with me—give more meaning to every chapter, passage, or verse He chooses to speak over me. Knowing His covenant with me is the same one God made with Abraham gives extra power to the words in Isaiah 43:1 when He says, in essence, "I created you, I formed you, I redeemed you."

The Bible is alive and active, ready to speak to us about any circumstance or situation that we're praying about.

The authority of the Bible as ex-plained through this study gives it present-day power to speak instruc-tion or comfort to me. When I turn the pages of this study manual with the blanks filled in so many years ago, I'm reminded of the revelations we received just by studying the Bible in its entirety. Which is a good reason to continue doing Bible studies at every age, in every season.

Some treat the Bible as a history book or a collection of interest-ing stories. It is that, but it's so much more! The Bible is alive and active, ready to speak to us about any circumstance or situation that we're praying about. Having a good understanding of the Book, its chapters, and specific stories will also help us. Without the context of the new covenant, we're tempted to believe that these stories were just for saints of old. Knowing that I'm in covenant with the same God who answered Abraham gives me assurance that He will speak just as clearly to me.

Angels to the NSEW

Being familiar with the Bible, the active and alive instruction book from God to us, helps us recognize the answers God is providing to our prayers. I always pray for protection over our family members when they are traveling with this repeated phrase: "Praying angels to the north, south, east, and west of you." The longer version of this is found in Psalm 91:11–12:

> For he will command his angels concerning you
> to guard you in all your ways;
> they will lift you up in their hands,
> so that you will not strike your foot against a stone.

This answer to me on how to pray for protection seems to be stated so clearly with the phrase "to guard you in all your ways" that it covers a variety of possible bad scenarios floating in this mom's brain. I shortened it many years ago to the NSEW version, partly so that I could remember it and partly because when I'm praying over our family members after they've packed the car and are ready to leave the driveway, a quicker version makes everyone happier.

Sixteen years ago Jess and a friend were leaving our house after a day spent trying on wedding dresses. They were in a hurry to get back to college in Columbia, South Carolina, but I insisted on praying over them before they left. We got a frantic call from Jess about an hour later, saying they had a wreck and the car was totaled but everyone was okay. As we drove that long hour on the interstate to meet them, we saw the car she had been driving. The car had spun several times, caught in a high wind, then crashed into a massive steel frame that supported the interstate exit sign. We cried and hugged as we found the girls at a nearby convenience store, and Jess's first words to me were: "I'll never complain about you praying angels to the NSEW again." Truly, they were protected from more than their feet hitting a rock.

More recently I was praying for our daughter Caroline as she was traveling on vacation in Iceland. I didn't know anything about Iceland except that it's an island of green spaces and ice off the coast of Europe in the huge Iceland Sea. Caroline and her travel friend had problems with their rental car, resulting in four hours on the side of the road with a mechanic. Once the car was fixed, they proceeded on their route following the ring road around the southern tip of the country, but the delay meant they were now traveling late at night. She texted and asked for prayer because it would be after midnight when they arrived at their destination. Oh, and it was snowing. With all those factors in a country terrain I couldn't envision, the only thing I knew to pray was, "Lord, please put angels to the north, south, east, and west of these girls." The next text I got from Caroline read: "We only had one hour to go, but a sweet lady saw us pulled over at a fork in the road and gave us advice. The way our map was taking us was a 'shortcut' that was unpaved mountain roads. She encouraged us to instead take the longer route along the ocean road."

Caroline had already shared with me how friendly the people of Iceland are, but this was at eleven at night. For there to be a woman at the very time they needed advice, at the very place, at that hour of the night, in the snow . . . had to be an angel. I'm thankful for this short, pithy prayer based on Scripture that reminds me to ask God for angels and be thankful for all the times they have protected us.

Pick a Bible, Any Bible

The most incredible thing to me about getting familiar with the Bible is how many options we have during this specific time in history. I can remember as a sixteen-year-old being so excited to have a paperback version called *The Way*, which was filled with devotions and pictures specifically made for high schoolers. The words of the New Testament leapt off each page as I devoured the stories in a different format. Even then it was paperback and only included the New Testament.

Later as a young mom, I enjoyed the *Women's Devotional Bible* because the devotions sprinkled throughout the Bible spoke to my season of life. During a season of learning and increased interest in a more in-depth version, I used the *Amplified Bible* as my go-to. Later, I chose a study Bible because the summary notes at the beginning of each book and study notes on each page gave me ways to search other cross-referenced Scriptures for context.

During my current season of Bible learning, I lean toward using my online Bible via YouVersion because I can copy and paste into the journal pages of my iPad as I'm exploring a passage. I also love *The Bible Recap* by Tara-Leigh Cobble and refer to my Kindle version of it often. There are limitless options today, whether you want a hefty printed copy of the Bible or a digital version.

It's such a gift to have so many options and ways to read the Book, so we can be prepared when there's an open-book test. That test might be a difficult season you're walking through, and a chapter or several chapters will guide you as you walk through the fire and through the floods. Or maybe you're needing some help from God's Word on how to pray for a specific need. With the added benefit of Google, you just need to be familiar enough to recall a few words in a passage to locate the reference. So what are we waiting for? The answers are in the Book! Let's pick a version and start reading!

ASK in Your Life

1. What verse from the Bible resonates with you during this season? Maybe you've heard it in a song or in a sermon or even here in this book. Write it down and meditate on what it means for you.

2. Like the shortened version of Psalm 91:11–12, "Praying angels to the north, south, east, and west of you," what passage from the Bible do you like to pray over specific situations? If you don't have a Scripture prayer, find one and claim it as your own!

3. Have you ever experienced God's protection in a situation and wondered if it was an angel? The next time you or a loved one comes through a near tragedy unscathed, consider whether God may have sent you an angel.

4. Which version of the Bible are you reading most consistently? Try a different translation to give yourself a new perspective.

CHAPTER 18

WHEN PEACE
IS AN ANSWER

While many times God answers our asks with a door that swings wide open or a quiet whisper suddenly dropped into our thought life, there is another way He answers that is more subtle. Maybe you've heard other Christians say, "I just had peace about the decision." If you haven't experienced it yourself, you might think they were talking in riddles. It's a real experience to feel peace, and it's also biblical. Let's explore what it means to feel peace as an answer to your ask.

The Peace of Christ

Since we're dealing with a tricky subject seemingly tied to emotions rather than intellect, let's go directly to the source: Jesus. We know that Jesus exhibited peace in many situations when He walked on earth, right?

He was accused and sought after by the Pharisees and the Jewish rulers because they were afraid of his growing popularity. Yet Jesus was at peace.

He was surrounded by disciples who loved Him and had the benefit of His personal teachings while still competing for a place of honor next to Him. Yet Jesus was at peace.

Even though Jesus expressed rebuke at times, He did it without losing control or sinning in His anger.

After being in great anguish in Gethsemane, praying for deliverance and sweating drops of blood, Jesus still emerged from the garden at peace. While some of His followers exhibited anger and an eagerness to fight, Jesus was at peace with the Father's will: "Look, the hour has come, and the Son of Man is delivered into the hands of sinners. Rise! Let us go! Here comes my betrayer!" (Matthew 26:45–46).

This is why Jesus is my role model for peace. If His supernatural peace amid trials and death is too much for us to hope for, we can at the very least understand the peace that comes from Christ: "Let the peace of Christ rule in your hearts, since as members of one body you were called to peace" (Colossians 3:15). The Greek word for "rule" in this verse is *brabeuo*,[14] which is an athletic term meaning "to act as the arbiter in games, to umpire." So we are reminded here that even though inward emotions like fear, anger, or turmoil arise when circumstances are difficult, we are to umpire or rule over those emotions with the peace of Christ.

If you haven't ever experienced the peace of Christ, this will sound elusive, so let's look at another explanation. In his article "3 Ways God Will Give You Confirmation," Mark Ballenger explains it this way:

> **When You Are Making the Right Decision, You Will Experience Biblical Emotions as Confirmation.**
>
> Emotions should not be our only guide in life. But the Bible does tell us that we will experience certain emotions when we are following God's will for our lives (perhaps none more prevalent than peace). Emotions like peace (Philippians 4:7), joy (Philippians 4:4), and contentment (Philippians 4:11–13) are signs that you truly are doing what God wants you to do.

These emotions don't always come right away. Sometimes we need to make hard decisions that will cause us to feel anxiety or even fear at first. But once you obey the Lord, the Bible promises us that we will experience the supernatural peace and love of the Holy Spirit that surpasses human understanding.[15]

Peace with a No

It's always easier to have peace with a closed door or a no answer with the perspective that time brings. I can look back over decades of job applications that didn't result in the job and see where it was for my good. Careers that seemed like the dream at first would've caused me to climb a corporate ladder instead of pursuing God's best for my life. City relocations or home choices or even churches we attended became pivotal points of connection for our family.

When a no answer doesn't bring peace, our trust in God leads us to remember Jesus's parting gift and promise. After the Last Supper, Jesus gave final instructions to the disciples: "All this I have spoken while still with you. But the Advocate, the Holy Spirit, whom the Father will send in my name, will teach you all things and will remind you of everything I have said to you. Peace I leave with you; my peace I give you. I do not give to you as the world gives. Do not let your hearts be troubled and do not be afraid" (John 14:25–27). So even when we don't see the ultimate good, we have the Holy Spirit, our Advocate, to help us find the peace Christ gave to us.

> Even when we don't see the ultimate good, we have the Holy Spirit, our Advocate, to help us find the peace Christ gave to us.

Peace with a Yes

When our oldest grandchild, AnnaJaye Walters, was deciding on which college to attend, Gibson and I were honored to take her on one college visit while her parents were working. I'll never forget the excitement that came after that visit when she experienced the peace of God's answer. She had already visited three other colleges, and while they each had pros and cons, none of them felt like where God was calling her to undergraduate work. We went on a short tour of the campus with AnnaJaye and were impressed with how they were recruiting her, not just for Bible college but also to play basketball. Since the other colleges had also given her the VIP treatment, this didn't faze AnnaJaye, so we left for a few hours to let her explore and meet some of the faculty and students.

When we returned that afternoon, her face was glowing with excitement, and she talked nonstop on the two-hour trip back to Charleston. The finances were daunting for this private university, but I knew from the peace in her spirit that this would be AnnaJaye's number one choice. She actually said, "Nonny, I just feel such peace about this being the right college for me." When I asked AnnaJaye to describe more about that feeling of peace, she offered the following explanation:

> Spiritual peace is a very dynamic thing, but as a believer, the peace of God gets to rule our hearts (Philippians 4:7). So if it's guarding or ruling our hearts, it should encompass every decision we make if we're walking with Christ. But especially in those moments of big decisions, when we are really earnest to know how to move forward, the peace of God rules my heart. What I found out at the other colleges was not necessarily a scream of "This is not for you," but I never heard Him say "This is for you" like I did on this university visit. When I can really attach a decision to the peace of God and walking in intimacy with God, there is usually also a next step, and the next step becomes irrevocable. I knew that I couldn't have

avoided taking the next steps with this university (talking to my parents, applying, obtaining funding), and I also couldn't have mustered my way through them on my own.

Peace is a freedom from disturbance, with no emotional conflicts within yourself or with other people. There were no conflicts within AnnaJaye, and the resulting emotion was peace. She could see herself in the classrooms and on the basketball court. She could see her future days at this university. It wasn't the swag of T-shirts, posters, and printed material that influenced her but the peace Jesus gave by linking hearts with a people and a place. When God calls us to a people and a place, He gives us peace.

Peace with a Goodbye

After I'd served in a church body of women for ten years, saying goodbye to the calling of full-time ministry was difficult to say the least. My last weekend of working was also Mother's Day, so I had been asked to speak on a panel of women for all the weekend services. While I knew God was calling me to better balance family and ministry, I didn't have a clear picture of what that next step would look like. Trading in the security of a well-established ministry with leaders and women I loved dearly was harder than trading in the security of a paycheck. But I knew God had spoken clearly, and it was time to step out on that precipice.

During the first of four services that weekend, after I finished speaking, the band and singers came to the stage to lead us in worship. Our songs were always contemporary and upbeat, so you can imagine my surprise when one of the last songs was "Standing on the Promises." My daughter Katie had mentioned to the worship leader that this was a favorite of mine, and the band put together a special rendition of it for that weekend. This song was one that my church ensemble, the St. Andrews Singers, had sung together back in the late eighties when we toured, and I knew every word by heart:

189

Standing, standing,
Standing on the promises of God my Savior;
Standing, standing,
I'm standing on the promises of God.

The lines that were always so comforting to me were now on the projection screens, and I sang them mightily, with tears streaming down my face:

Standing on the promises I shall not fall,
List'ning every moment to the Spirit's call,
Resting in my Savior as my all in all,
Standing on the promises of God.

God's peace over my next step, and the call on my life, had just come in the way of song lyrics.

Peace like a River

As I've written before, songs and lyrics have always been an important part of my life, and I'm sure God knows that is a good way to talk to me. In my late twenties, I had the joy of singing in a church choir with my dad, and sometimes we would harmonize at home beside the piano. One of his favorite hymns that became one of mine was "It Is Well with My Soul." The story of this hymn's author, Horatio Spafford, was part of what made it our favorite.

Spafford had two traumatic events in his life initially, the death of his four-year-old son and being ruined financially in the Great Chicago Fire of 1871. Just a couple of years later in 1873, Spafford was planning to travel to England with his family, but in a last-minute delay due to business, he sent them ahead. While crossing the Atlantic, the family's ship sank after colliding with another vessel, and all four of Spafford's daughters died. Soon after as Spafford was traveling that same passage to join his grieving wife, he wrote this song while passing over the place where his daughters died.

These are the original lyrics:

> When peace like a river attendeth my way,
> When sorrows like sea billows roll;
> Whatever my lot, Thou hast taught me to say
> It is well, it is well with my soul.
>
> It is well (it is well)
> With my soul (with my soul).

Spafford had suffered some of life's greatest sorrows in just a few short years: the death of all five of his children and financial collapse. Yet his trust in God reminded him that it was well with his soul. He knew that circumstances don't bring peace; only trust in a sovereign God will.

My dad passed away at an early age when I was just thirty-eight years old, and I've missed him over the past twenty-five-plus years. But the words from our favorite hymn taught me about peace like a river, in death and in life, and about a much greater peace in Christ that helps me discern God's voice.

Find Your Peace

Still wondering how to feel the peace of Christ over an answer or a decision from God? Maybe songs and lyrics aren't your soul's voice and God will give you the confirmation of peace in another way. Are you an artist or a creative? He may choose something visually that will confirm a Scripture and give you peace. Perhaps you are a teacher and God will use an illustrative story to give you peace about an ask. He is a creative God and will use ways that are specific to your personality and your wiring. The most critical part is to know what peace feels like, and when you are in the midst of an ask, to be ready for God to show you the peace that will confirm His answers.

ASK in Your Life

1. How does the "peace of Christ" mentioned in Colossians 3:15 and the Greek meaning of that phrase help you to grow in living more like Jesus?

2. Memorize John 14:27 and write it down where you will see it often. Read this verse over your soul the next time you feel anxious or worried.

3. When have you experienced peace in making a big decision, like when AnnaJaye was choosing which college to attend? If you haven't experienced this peace, how can you apply the principles from her story to your next decision?

4. In what ways does God give you peace when pursuing His best? How is this linked to how you're wired (i.e., creative, musician, writer, parent, accountant)? Brainstorm a list of ways God might give you peace.

CHAPTER 19

ANSWERS WE SEE IN A LIFETIME

Some answers to prayer are seen immediately, and they build our faith in God. Other answers have long-term effects that aren't seen for decades. Certainly there are days when injustice or heartache leaves us doubting if God is hearing our asks. On those days we cry out like the prophet Habakkuk:

> How long, LORD, must I call for help,
>   but you do not listen?
> Or cry out to you, "Violence!"
>   but you do not save?
> Why do you make me look at injustice?
>   Why do you tolerate wrongdoing? (1:2–3)

One aspect of the Israelite people that I find noteworthy in the Old Testament is how the people of God continued to tell their children stories of His faithfulness. They didn't have laptops or internet or social media, but they told the stories of their ancestors to their children. Their history was preserved by their storytelling culture and then eventually written down for us to read today.

When we read their stories of victory in battle or God's rescue from floods, fires, seas, or drought, we are encouraged. This was the benefit of their telling the stories and handing down the testimonies to the next generation, as they were also encouraged in their faith.

So what of the victories God has done in our lives? If we fail to tell the stories or mark the testimonies, they will be forgotten. "Aaron Holt of the National Archives and Records Administration says that 'it only takes three generations to lose a piece of oral family history.' If you want to avoid losing those precious family stories passed down through the generations, Holt continued, the story 'must be purposely and accurately repeated over and over again through the generations to be preserved.'"[16] If we are to preserve the history of our faith, we need to tell the rescue stories of God to future generations.

Modern-Day Storytelling

One way to keep our stories of God's faithfulness is to write them down in a journal, a document, or a book to be shared after we pass to heaven. Telling our stories to our children and grandchildren is also powerful, but unless we tell them again and again, there's a chance they won't remember by the time they are adults. There are many times I regret not getting more written histories from my mother and father, but they died when I was still in the thick of a full and busy life.

Another way to mark the testimonies that our family has found helpful is taken from 1 Samuel 7. At the beginning of this chapter, we learn that the prophet Samuel finally gave an ultimatum to all the house of Israel and told them to put away their foreign gods and return to the Lord, serving Him only. He promised that if they put away their Baals and Ashtoreths, God would protect them from the Philistines. They agreed and gathered at Mizpah to acknowledge their sin before God. But the Philistines heard they were gathered at

Mizpah, and they prepared to go against them. The Israelites heard of the upcoming attack and were afraid, begging Samuel to continue crying out to God on their behalf. Samuel offered a lamb as a burnt offering to the Lord, and God answered. When the Philistines were approaching, the Lord thundered with a mighty sound that threw them into confusion, and they were defeated by Israel. To make sure that the Israelites marked this momentous day and remembered how God saved them, Samuel set up a memorial stone, which he called Ebenezer: "Then Samuel took a stone and set it up between Mizpah and Shen. He named it Ebenezer, saying, 'Thus far the LORD has helped us'" (v. 12).

In 2018 Gibson and I were celebrating our twenty-fifth anniversary, and we wanted to have a rededication of our vows in the backyard, surrounded by family and friends. It was a beautiful ceremony led by our two pastor sons-in-law and our three daughters, with all the grandchildren in attendance. We wanted the occasion to also provide a marker of a different sort, so we used that day to build a wall of "Ebenezers" around our small garden pond.

What we tried to capture on those stones were the answers to prayers we have experienced thus far, much like Samuel did. Obvious answers to prayer were memorialized with a stone for the birth of each of our three daughters, the marriages to the two sons-in-law, and the birth of each grandchild. Other stones were placed to mark God's healing of Jess's meningitis and Glory's healing from seizures. Some stones marked friendships God brought into our lives, like my friend Kay Sumner. It was a fun time during our ceremony to let the grandchildren place their stones on the wall, and I've found them in the years since, going back to find their named stones.

We add a few stones every year, and one Thanksgiving we added one for our oldest grandchild, AnnaJaye Walters, receiving a basketball scholarship to college, along with some professional milestones of our adult daughters. By calling these Ebenezers instead of just accomplishments, we are acknowledging that no answer to prayer is possible in our lives without God's help.

Hindsight Is Often God Sight

Sometimes we don't see the full impact of answered prayers—or the ways God has intervened and directed our paths—for many years or even decades. However, if we're faithful to note answered prayers along the way, then hindsight makes it easier to spot the interventions of God. The saying "hindsight is twenty-twenty" is usually quoted to remind us that it's always easier to see a solution in hindsight. But I like to flip that around with the idea that "hindsight is God sight." This acknowledges when we're able to connect the dots of an answered prayer to a bigger picture. It's not often that we have God's sight in perceiving the greater impact, but it's so illuminating when we do.

Sometimes we don't see the full impact of answered prayers— or the ways God has intervened and directed our paths— for many years or even decades.

One time we saw the greater impact of God's answer to an ask sooner than years or decades—in fact, it was within a few months of the answer. I've told the story of our move from Charlotte to Charleston. There were many facets of that answered ask, but one had some longer-reaching benefits. When Gibson followed God's leading in accepting the job with the Navy that December, he learned that they wanted him to come to work as soon as possible. That wasn't ideal because we still had a house to sell in Charlotte, and this was during a stalled real estate season. We also had two daughters still at home, and Jess was a senior who would be graduating from high school six months later in June. Katie was a sophomore at the University of South Carolina (USC), so the move didn't affect her. But both Gibson and I were being paid severances that finished in December, so we agreed moving sooner rather than later seemed ideal. While we were praying about the right timing for this move, we looked at the calendar and Gibson picked the date of January 13 to start work, knowing his new employer would provide him temporary residence until we could join later.

Here's where the "God sight" gets interesting. We had been paying out-of-state tuition for Katie to attend USC, and Jess had indicated she would like to go there—but we didn't see any way our budget could accommodate two of those hefty tuitions. A few months after Gibson started his new job, I visited the bursar's office at USC to start paperwork for future in-state tuition. The woman helping me took my proof of residency. Then she told me it was retroactive if my husband had been working in the state on or before the first day of the semester. When was the first day of that semester? January 13 of course! We saw this as an immediate pay increase because of in-state tuition, and now we even had a refund coming. It also paved the way for Jess to apply and attend there the following year. Coincidence? No. I believe it was God sight prompting Gibson to choose a start date that would bless our family in the midst of his obedience to provide for us, even when it meant living in a hotel room for months. Seeking God in prayer helped Gibson choose exactly the right start date, even when we didn't have insight about all the far-reaching implications. Within months, God sight showed us that He was in the details of our family move.

God Sight for the Generations

Other "hindsight is God sight" moments happen over longer periods of time—sometimes decades. I've already mentioned that one of my greatest prayers for our children from birth was that they would walk with God. Sometime during their teenage years, I realized that praying for godly spouses should be my next priority ASK for each daughter. So I began to pray for each of their future spouses, trusting God with providing exactly who they each needed for a life partner.

It isn't lost on me that our choices impact those of our children and generations to come in a multifaceted way. For example, when

I married Gibson, I married into a family of USC alumni and fans. This doesn't sound like a big deal since we only lived ninety miles from USC, but we lived in the Tar Heel State. Living in Charlotte, almost all our friends and family attended North Carolina universities, and it wasn't the norm for students to leave a Charlotte high school and go across the state line. In those first few years of marriage, we took Katie to a USC game, and she was captivated. It doesn't take super sight to recognize that without Gibson's influence, she wouldn't have gone to USC, and that was where she met her husband, Josh Walters. That's a generational impact times seven since they now have seven children whose lives are the direct result of God leading and guiding Gibson, the USC Gamecock, to me.

Taking that hindsight even further, God leading us to relocate to Charleston has had more impact than we could have ever imagined. Katie and Josh lived in Columbia after graduating from college and started their ministry and teaching careers there. We drove the two hours frequently for celebrations, especially once the grandchildren were born. They also came to visit us and loved visiting the church we attended. About five years into their marriage and ministry, I started sending Josh CDs of weekend sermons from Seacoast Church to encourage him. He was a youth pastor in Columbia and didn't have strong leadership pouring into him at the time.

When they knew it was time to leave Columbia, they moved to Charleston, and Josh began discipling under one of those Seacoast pastors, in part because of all the teaching CDs he had listened to. Within a year Josh was on staff with the Kidscoast ministry team and worked through several department leadership roles. Now he serves on the executive team at Seacoast Church and is one of the teaching pastors who preaches to over twenty-five thousand people on a weekend. Katie was able to start her nonprofit benefiting women and children in Togo because she went on a Seacoast mission trip to Togo and felt a passion to help those with little means of providing for themselves and their children. Her nonprofit, Francis + Benedict, is now a wide-reaching organization employing eleven seamstresses in

Togo and over two hundred advocates in the United States. God's sight to plant the Walters in Charleston has had far-reaching effects that go way beyond them moving to be near us.

Our middle daughter, Jess, met her husband, Nick Connolly, because of another God sight. When we lived in Charlotte, Jess experienced a spiritual revival on a weekend retreat and asked us to consider going to another church where she could have more Bible study and accountability. Gibson and I prayed about it for several months and felt the Lord leading us to visit a church in our neighborhood. After we all went there for several Sundays, Jess wasn't convinced it was what she was looking for, but Gibson and I felt the Holy Spirit leading us there. Within a few months, Jess found connection and was in a high school girl's small group that met weekly for accountability. A year later she went on a mission trip to Brazil and met Nick Connolly. When they got married in their senior year at USC, they settled in Charlotte to pursue careers and serve in a church there.

Ten years later, after living in several other states and Nick completing seminary, they felt called to start a church here in Charleston. They planted Bright City Church, which now serves hundreds in downtown Charleston and ministers to many who are looking for just this type of church. Another God sight of them settling here is that Jess formed a global missional organization, Go and Tell Gals, which coaches and trains women to use their gifts for the good of others, with a staff of six and an office in downtown Charleston. Could God have accomplished this church and this organization in another city if they hadn't moved here? Probably, but the way He lined up their passions and ministries with other people located here makes us call an audible on this being a God sight.

Here I Raise My Ebenezer

So we are left with this question: What can we do to continue the stories of God's remarkable answers to our prayers so they aren't lost within three generations? One thing I'm trying to do is write more letters and cards. The handwritten ones I have from my mother and mother-in-law are such a treasure, and I want my family members to have more than just my Instagram feed to remember. Maybe you have the gift of storytelling and will bring it back to future generations by telling the stories of how God rescued and answered you. We can all become better listeners as others tell those stories, especially when we connect our stories to the power of God. Maybe you will consider putting up an Ebenezer wall like ours or an Ebenezer memorial! In any form, let's commit to raising an Ebenezer!

> Come Thou fount of every blessing;
> Tune my heart to sing Thy grace;
> Streams of mercy, never ceasing,
> Call for songs of loudest praise.
> Teach me some melodious sonnet,
> Sung by flaming tongues above;
> Praise the mount, I'm fixed upon it,
> Mount of Thy redeeming love!
>
> Here I raise my Ebenezer;
> Here by Thy great help I've come;
> And I hope by Thy good pleasure
> Safely to arrive at home.

ASK in Your Life

1. What are some practical ways to mark Ebenezers in your life? List them in a journal or on a notepad. Think about how a visible marker would help your family members see and hear about God's imprint on your life.

2. How does the principle that "hindsight is God sight" help you connect the dots for some answers in your life? If you can't think of a God sight in your past, try writing down the details of an ongoing ASK to track the results later.

3. How can you include more storytelling in your times around the dinner table or with your community? Jot down a few stories and ask God to sharpen the details for the next time you're gathering with others. Or focus on listening to the stories of your elders and ask strategic questions to encourage their storytelling.

CHAPTER 20

THINGS SEEN IN GENERATIONS TO COME

Even if we keep our eyes wide open, walk in the power of the Holy Spirit, and memorialize every answered prayer with an Ebenezer, we're still going to miss some of God's finest work. Our view is too myopic, and our time on earth is too limited. Some of His answers won't reach fruition for generations to come, and others we won't celebrate until heaven. Why is this so hard for us to comprehend or accept?

There was a period of my life when I paid more attention to signs and symbols of astrology than understanding and applying God's Word. Why was it so easy for me to trust the unseen world of astrology rather than people of past generations who prayed for me? Maybe because I could identify with the bland descriptors, and the predictions are relatable. We all want to feel seen and secure in our future.

I believe the unseen world of prayers offered on our behalf, decades and even centuries ago, is more powerful than how the stars aligned in the month of our birth. How am I so sure? Maybe it's my age and length of time on planet Earth that gives me a glimpse of the power of the prayers of those who came before me. I know that I am reaping the benefits of prayers offered up by my grandparents and perhaps countless other ancestors.

Ottie and Papa

My paternal grandparents were Olive and Ernest Powell, but their grandparent names, Ottie and Papa, became their fond nicknames for most everyone who knew them in the sixties and seventies. I have a treasure trove of memories growing up with the extended Powell family, from summer vacations at the beach or mountains to Sunday afternoons watching golf for hours and then *Walt Disney's Wonderful World of Color*. Papa Powell was truly a self-made man, dropping out of school at thirteen to support his family and then going back to night school for his GED. From cleaning looms in a cotton mill on Saturdays for fifty cents a loom, he progressively rose up in leadership of this mill in Anderson, South Carolina. Later he was asked by the mill owners to move to Charlotte and supervise a chain of mills in both states.

Papa was humble, quiet-spoken, and generous with his family. Not only was he generous with vacations and gifts, but he generously spoke words of life and belief in our futures over each of us ten grandchildren. At one point in my later teens, he pulled me aside and said, "God has big plans for you, Debbie." His words grew a desire in me to never settle, to love deeply, and to share freely with others.

Although he never prayed aloud for us individually, we heard him pray as he led the family before each meal or celebration. He was faithful in the local church and served in ways much like his personality, quietly and behind the scenes.

But it was my grandmother Ottie's prayers I felt the most then and feel most today. Ottie never worked after marriage, and she also never got her driver's license. Despite not driving, she attended a women's prayer circle weekly and was faithful to attend all Sunday church services. Most importantly, Ottie was a prayer warrior. She kept her daily devotions private, and her prayers were much the same, but we knew she prayed for our safety and for us to love God. We knew she was praying over each member of our family. Though she might've worried about some of our wayward paths in the sixties and seventies, she released those worries in prayer to our heavenly Father. She went to heaven before my children were born, but I know she is able to see the generations who followed from her fervent prayer life.

Infidels and Earthquakes

One of my hobbies is ancestry, and it's fascinating to read about the men and women in our family history. While I like filling in the dates and lineage, the real joy is when I read a story or a document sharing more about their personalities and their everyday lives. Sometimes it's only a small thread to pull, but I love to take those threads and ask God to show me more.

One of these threads is from the life of my second-great-grand-mother, Mary Brown Hall Powell. Mary was born in 1840 and married Thomas Almon Powell when she was seventeen. A note written by my great-uncle Ed Powell in our 150-year family history album he compiled reads: "Mary Hall Powell rode her horse side-saddle to church. One Sunday, her horse could not be used and she used a different horse which threw her and broke her leg. She died later since doctors at that time did not know what to do for a broken leg."

While I'm sad that she died at the young age of forty-three, leaving five children and two stepdaughters, I'm encouraged that she was faithful to her local church. So faithful that a sick or wounded horse didn't stop her from attending! That's the kind of praying woman I know was in my ancestry. I'm thankful for Mary and her prayers and believe they have impacted us and many generations to come.

Later in that same family history album, I found why Mary was attending church alone. Two lines of text are rich with understanding and confirmation that she was praying for those who would live after her death: "Thomas Almon Powell (Mary's widower husband) would

not go to church since he was an infidel. One day there was an earthquake (1886) and Thomas was very frightened. His son, William Powell, heard him in the next room praying for God to take care of them."

I'm not sure if the earthquake put the fear of God into Thomas
enough for him to be saved, but it surely made an impact on young
William, who was fifteen at the time. William later served God faithfully by playing the organ every week in church, and one of his and
Louise's ten children would become my papa. If an infidel could
produce a mighty man of God like Papa, then Mary's prayers were
powerful and effective. "The heartfelt and persistent prayer of a righ-
teous man (believer) can accomplish much [when put into action
and made effective by God—it is dynamic and can have tremendous
power]" (James 5:16 AMP).

Mother Ruth

When I think about my ancestors who prayed for future generations, I think about Ruth. Ruth's husband died during a famine,
and she made the hard choice to leave her people and her land with
her mother-in-law because of her faith in God. As a young widow,
her chances for remarriage were slim, but with the guidance of her
mother-in-law, Naomi, and God's favor, Ruth married Boaz. Boaz
provided for both of them and their future children. The first child?
Let's read the text:

> So Boaz took Ruth and she became his wife. When he
> made love to her, the LORD enabled her to conceive, and
> she gave birth to a son. The women said to Naomi: "Praise
> be to the LORD, who this day has not left you without a
> guardian-redeemer. May he become famous throughout
> Israel! He will renew your life and sustain you in your old
> age. For your daughter-in-law, who loves you and who is
> better to you than seven sons, has given him birth."
>
> Then Naomi took the child in her arms and cared for
> him. The women living there said, "Naomi has a son!"

And they named him Obed. He was the father of Jesse, the father of David. (Ruth 4:13–17)

Because of Ruth's obedience and faith, she birthed a son who would be the grandfather to King David. More importantly, she is listed in the lineage of Jesus. Mother Ruth, a devoted woman of God, was the ancestor of a king and our King! Do we have written prayers she prayed for David and for Jesus? No, we don't. The same way I'm not certain of the specific words that my Ottie Powell or Mary Powell prayed for me and our family. But I'm confident that any woman of faith who loved God prayed not just for herself but for those she loved and for those who would follow in future generations. Likewise, it's important for us to see the impact of the praying women who came before us and take up the same mantle of generational prayer.

It's important for us to take up the mantle of generational prayer.

Our Shared Intercessor

What if your ancestors weren't Christians or people of prayer and you're the first in a long line of unbelievers? The greatest comfort we can take is that we all share the highest and most powerful intercessor ever known—Jesus! When He was about to be betrayed, Jesus didn't pray for His own rescue from certain death. He prayed for each one of us:

> My prayer is not for them alone. I pray also for those who will believe in me through their message, that all of them may be one, Father, just as you are in me and I am in you. May they also be in us so that the world may believe that you have sent me. I have given them the glory that you

gave me, that they may be one as we are one—I in them
and you in me—so that they may be brought to complete
unity. (John 17:20–23)

If He prayed these words for us in His darkest hour, we can only
imagine what Jesus is praying for each one of us now.

The Upper Side

Whether we see the direct impact of generational prayers by those in
our past, or by our highest intercessor, Jesus, we can be confident that
all will be revealed to us in heaven. I've long been a fan of the poem
called "The Weaver" by Grant Colfax Tullar. When I think about God
as the Weaver, these words remind me that we often don't see the
meaning or reasons for the steps and missteps in our life, but He sees
the upper side of the tapestry. When we join Him in heaven for eternity, I'm not sure if we'll see a slideshow or movie of our lives, but I
look forward to seeing the revealed tapestry:

> My Life is but a weaving
> Between my Lord and me;
> I cannot choose the colors
> He worketh steadily.
>
> Oft times He weaveth sorrow
> And I, in foolish pride,
> Forget He sees the upper,
> And I the underside. . . .
>
> The dark threads are as needful
> In the Weaver's skillful hand,
> As the threads of gold and silver
> In the pattern He has planned.[17]

Our view is too shortsighted and our prayers even more so. If we
could just pray with the faithfulness of the prayer warriors who have

gone before us, we might not see prayers answered here on earth but would see great rewards in heaven. Maybe it's because Papa Powell cleaned weaving looms that I'm particularly drawn to this verse of the poem:

> Not till the loom is silent
> And the shuttles cease to fly,
> Shall God unroll the canvas
> And explain the reason why.

The loom is still very busy weaving the tapestry or canvas of our lives and generations to come. Let us never make prayer too complicated or too cumbersome. Instead let us simply pray—asking, seeking, and knocking—and trust the answers to the Weaver.

ASK in Your Life

1. Who in your family line (parents, grandparents, or even previous generations) prayed for you or is praying for you? If you aren't sure, ask your older family members.
2. Memorize James 5:16 and ask God how you might put fervent prayer into action.
3. Read the book of Ruth and then trace her lineage in Matthew 1. How does this lineage of prayer encourage you to pray for future generations?
4. Read John 17:20–23, then write it down, inserting your name every time the passage says "they" or "them." Read that over yourself as a powerful reminder that Jesus is praying for you.

LET PRAYER
BE YOUR SUPERPOWER

led a small group last year that met on Tuesday afternoons. Because we were accommodating working women who could join during their lunch hour, I was very intentional with our one hour starting and ending on time. One Tuesday when we ended at 1 p.m. on the dot, my daughter Jess looked over at me and said, "Ending on time is your superpower!"

Initially I was happy with that since logistics seems to be one of my giftings. I love a to-do list, an agenda, a plan, or anything that contributes to efficiency. My family looks to me for logistics, and I'm great with that too. But when I left small group that day, I began having the meeting after the meeting in my head and thought, I don't want efficiency to be my superpower. I don't want ending on time to be my superpower. At the end of my days on earth, I don't want the words spoken about me or my legacy to be "Deb always ended her meetings on time."

So the next question I asked myself was, What is a superpower anyway? Since we have seven grandchildren who are boys, we watch a lot of superhero movies. I knew about shape-shifting, flying, spiderwebs against buildings, and being invisible. As I thought about all the Avengers movies we had watched, the one trait that all superheroes seem to have in common is that their superpower is not always visible. They look like normal people on the outside, but their superpower is the special strength that lies hidden until those powers are needed to get them—or someone else—out of trouble.

What Sustains You?

In writing this book, I'm reminded of just how many hard seasons I've been through in these sixtyish years of life:

- Teenage years with an alcoholic father
- First marriage ended in divorce after ten years
- Single-again years with girls ages three and six, living at almost poverty level
- Remarriage and the challenges that come with a blended family
- A sister in ICU and on a ventilator for three weeks
- A father with a leg amputation followed by a stroke, needing a wheelchair for eight years
- Job transitions and moves
- A mother with Parkinson's and dementia

During each of these hard seasons, I needed a rescue. While it would've been nice to have a superpower such as shape-shifting, the superpower that God used to save me time and time again was prayer.

It wasn't my timeliness or efficiency or logistics skills that saved me. It was prayer. Prayer that was mostly hidden under the surface for all those years. Prayer with my heavenly Father is what rescued me.

I hope that after reading some of my stories, you will see how God led me through asking, seeking, and knocking to receive answers in my greatest hours of need. Prayer has been part of my life since the age of eleven. Using the ASK model of prayer has been the superpower needed to reach out to God, who rescued me from the pit, redeemed me from my mistakes, and reminded me that He is on the throne when all seems lost.

Are You Ready?

How about you? Aren't you tired of trying to make it all happen? Aren't you weary of figuring out all the answers? Aren't you exhausted with trying to achieve, perform, and get it all right?

This passage always gives me relief:

> Are you tired? Worn out? Burned out on religion? Come to me. Get away with me and you'll recover your life. I'll show you how to take a real rest. Walk with me and work with me—watch how I do it. Learn the unforced rhythms of grace. I won't lay anything heavy or ill-fitting on you. Keep company with me and you'll learn to live freely and lightly. (Matthew 11:28–30 MSG)

If you walk with God and work with Him, using the simple principle of ask, seek, and knock can be your superpower. Let it be so deep in you that it won't matter if it's seen. Maybe no one will know that you pray regularly. Maybe no one will see your prayer journals. Certainly during my hard seasons, that I prayed wasn't readily apparent to others. But if you make prayer one of your consistent spiritual practices, it will show in the results of forward movement and the peaceful presence you bring to every environment and every situation. People will notice, and once you are confident in prayer, you can offer to pray for them.

When your days are done and your family gathers around to tell your legacy, they may not talk about how efficient you were. Or what a great cook you were. Or how well you organized the family calendar. But they will say, "She prayed for us. He spent time on his knees. She told me that she was praying for me. He texted me prayers and Scriptures. I felt their prayers. They made a difference. Prayer was their superpower."

Simply Pray

Let's do this. Let's start or recommit today! Pull out some index cards and write Matthew 7:7 on one side of each card: "Ask and it will be given to you; seek and you will find; knock and the door will be opened to you."

On the flip side of each card, write the one thing you are praying about. You can write the same thing on all the cards, or maybe you have several things like I did in my first ASK experience with my house, job, body, and car. Then for thirty days, post the cards where you only see the promise of Matthew 7:7 and release the problem to God. Keep your eyes open during those thirty days and look for ways that God will open doors for each situation. Jot down the moments when God is speaking or clarifying a question or opening a door so that you will have the testimony to encourage yourself and others.

If you remember anything from this book, my hope is it won't be a specific story or a funny anecdote. My prayer is you will remember a woman who was in a pit of despair, feeling alone and abandoned, who reached up toward God. I reached up with a few note cards and a Bible verse. Then God rescued me. And if He did it for me, He will do it for you!

It's easy to start. Just ASK. Simply pray.

ACKNOWLEDGMENTS

've long been a fan of the acknowledgments page, usually reading it before the introduction. Besides giving background on the author, it also gives insight into the people who provided motivation behind the work. Some people think writing is a solo sport. But anyone who has published knows it's a long game and can only be finished with a team of contributors.

My team starts with my family, for which I'm ever grateful. In 2020 during the COVID-19 pandemic, my daughter **Jess Connolly** nudged us to spend the vacuous days writing. She specifically poked me in saying, "Mom, I know you've got a book in you. You've been writing for years." Jess's encouragement didn't end there. She gave advice for coaches, proposals, and agents and was always available to answer questions—even while writing her eleventh book. She coaches women internationally, but this family coaching might be her best work ever. The result of this family's pandemic baby boom? Four of us are publishing in 2024 as first-time authors. Jess, I love your heart to champion everyone in your sphere of influence.

Her suggestions for an agent eventually led me to **Tom Dean**, who was literally an answer to one of my ASKs. I knew he was my guy when he said he'd need a couple of months to pray about signing me. Tom is a consistent communicator and advocate for his authors, at every stage of development. I'm looking forward to a long run with you, Tom, but not necessarily the eight-milers you complete daily.

Of course this book is about God and how I've seen Him move in my life, but I might never have made my first ASK to Him without my friend **Kay Johnson Smith**. Everyone needs a friend just a few steps ahead who's willing to be brutally honest and spiritually uplifting when you need it most. Kay, I know you keep an Ebenezer to our early days of Matthew 7:7 in your home. That says it all.

God knew I'd need another good friend to take this journey home, so when we moved to the low country He provided **Kay Sumner**. You've been faithful to check in on my writing process and encourage me when the road seemed long. Thank you for all the times you made me feel this was important to God, even as we browsed in a home goods store for candles.

So many other people behind the scenes sharpened and made my words better. The entire **Our Daily Bread Publishing team**, editor **Joel Armstrong**, and social media shadow **Emily Rypkema**, you've been patient but tough with this old bird, and I'm grateful for your leading.

I started with family and will end there. "The Fam" text thread keeps me going on hard days, and FaceTimes from daughters **Katie Walters** and **Caroline Hopper** are the wind beneath my wings. My husband and our Boaz, **Gibson Hopper**, is the one who pushed me through doubt toward next steps. You selflessly provided retreats for writing and ordered out when I was pushing a deadline. You've joked about wearing an ASK ball cap, but your support for this book is evident without it. Let's keep ASKing and raising Ebenezers for the rest of our days!

NOTES

1. *Merriam-Webster*, s.v. "avalanche (*n.*)," accessed April 3, 2023, https://www.merriam-webster.com/dictionary/avalanche.

2. "What Causes an Avalanche?," CBC News, September 24, 2012, https://www.cbc.ca/news/science/what-causes-an-avalanche-1.1174101.

3. Charles Spurgeon, *Spurgeon's Expositions of the Bible* (Omaha, NE: Patristic Publishing, 2019), 2773.

4. *Merriam-Webster*, s.v. "whatever (*pron.*)," accessed April 4, 2023, https://www.merriam-webster.com/dictionary/whatever.

5. Adrian Rogers, "Prayer and the Will of God," OnePlace, accessed April 19, 2023, https://www.oneplace.com/ministries/love-worth-finding/read/articles/prayer-and-the-will-of-god-11630.html.

6. *ESV Study Bible* (Wheaton, IL: Crossway, 2008).

7. "Statistics: Children and Divorce," Owenby Law, October 11, 2018, https://www.owenbylaw.com/blog/2018/october/statistics-children-divorce/.

8. Matthew Henry, "Matthew 7 Bible Commentary," *Matthew Henry Bible Commentary*, Christianity.com, accessed April 25, 2023, https://www.christianity.com/bible/commentary/matthew-henry-complete/matthew/7.

9. *Strong's Concordance*, s.v. "zéteó," BibleHub, accessed May 10, 2023, https://biblehub.com/greek/2212.htm.

10. Dictionary.com, s.v. "observe," accessed June 14, 2023, https://www.dictionary.com/browse/observe. Emphasis added.

11. Oswald Chambers, *My Utmost for His Highest*, ed. James Reimann (Grand Rapids, MI: Our Daily Bread Publishing, 1992), 365.

12. Dictionary.com, s.v. "observe," accessed May 1, 2023, https://www.dictionary.com/browse/observe.

13. John Gill, "Matthew 26:40," *Exposition of the Bible*, Bible Study Tools, accessed May 4, 2023, https://www.biblestudytools.com/commentaries/gills-exposition-of-the-bible/matthew-26-40.html.

14. *Strong's Concordance*, s.v. "*brabeuo*," Bible Hub, accessed June 16, 2023, https://biblehub.com/greek/1018.htm.

15. Mark Ballenger, "3 Ways God Will Give You Confirmation," Apply God's Word, February 6, 2020, https://applygodsword.com/3-ways-god-will-give-you-confirmation/.

16. Paul G. Nauta, "Oral Family History Fades in Just Three Generations," FamilySearch, May 19, 2014, https://www.familysearch.org/en/blog/oral-family-history-fades-in-just-three-generations.

17. "Grant Tullar, Music Publisher," *Bolton Community News*, August 2006, https://www.boltoncthistory.org/granttullar.html.

Spread the Word
by Doing One Thing.

- Give a copy of this book as a gift.
- Share the QR code link via your social media.
- Write a review of this book on your blog, favorite bookseller's website, or at ODB.org/store.
- Recommend this book to your church, small group, or book club.

Connect with us. 🅕 ⬡ 🐦

Our Daily Bread Publishing
PO Box 3566, Grand Rapids, MI 49501, USA
Email: books@odb.org

renew,
refresh,
reclaim

In a world that disappoints again and again, your
heavenly Father does not. Wherever you are
today and whatever your situation tomorrow,
know on a whole new level that God is with you,
He is for you, and He will never fail you.

Well-loved author, blogger, pastor's wife,
and women's ministry speaker Lori Hatcher
is here to help renew, refresh, and reclaim your
confidence in the rock-solid truths about God.

Our Daily Bread
Publishing®

Get yours today!

How do you deepen your relationship with and understanding of God?

At the source.
Get to know Him through His own Word, the Bible.

Know Him devotes 365 days to revealing the character of God solely through Scripture. These passages, drawn from every book of the Bible, highlight 12 unchanging attributes of our Creator. Whether you're new to the Bible or a longtime reader, you'll gain a deeper awe of God's holiness, transcendence, and glory along with a renewed appreciation for His mercy, justice, and truth.

Buy It Today

Our Daily Bread Publishing®

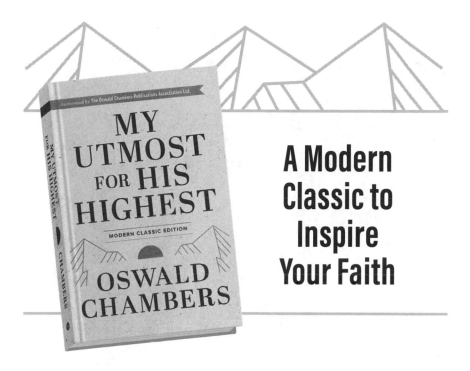

A Modern Classic to Inspire Your Faith

The timeless wisdom of Oswald Chambers shines in this new Modern Classic Edition of the beloved 365-day devotional first published by his widow in 1927. With a thoughtful approach to the language and context of the original, the author's voice has been carefully preserved and the Bible texts updated to the New International Version. Full of powerful challenges to devote your all for God's highest glory, these readings open the way to deeper, stronger faith.

Buy It Today

Love God. Love Others.

with  Our Daily Bread.

Your gift changes lives.

Connect with us. 📘 📷 🐦

Our Daily Bread Publishing
PO Box 3566, Grand Rapids, MI 49501, USA
Email: books@odb.org